Norman Weissman's lanovel. It is a loosely connected collection of ... various ways describe the futility of war and the use of force (deadly and subtle, national and sexual, individual and in groups) while chronicling the failure of democracy in Europe and the Middle East since the end of World War II. The stories are powerful and disturbing. They are also polemical. Polemical novels are out of vogue in the second decade of the 21st century, but they are part of a great tradition. Harriet Beecher Stowe, Charles Dickens, John Dos Passos, John Steinbeck, Upton Sinclair. Weissman has been unsparing in his portrayals of human cruelty and baseness. Weissman's book is a good read. He is a forceful writer. Before he is done with you, you have profound doubts about whether the generation born after World War II is creating a better world for their descendents."

Herman J. Obermayer, Author. *Soldiering For Freedom*: A G.I.'s account of World War II and *Rehnquist*, a personal portrait of the distinguished Chief Justice of the United States.

'A passionate and powerful story that shines a light on the futility of the endless use of violence to achieve anything, as violence begets more violence. A work of intellectual and emotional power relevant and timeless in its story and spirit. A wonderful book." Forrest Stone, MFA. Playwright. Yale School of Drama. Author. *No Sign After This Sign*.

"A staggering accomplishment. There are few artists who could compassionately and convincingly assemble such a suite of characters to illuminate our collective madness which expects a better world born from violence and demonization." Richard Geller. Author. *The Raspberry Man*.

"Incredibly beautiful! For three days now, upon awakening I have reached for your book, to be re-awakened to this world of pain and unsolvable contradictions. You write with eloquent precision, sensitive to the personal odyssey amid the sweeping tide of history. The blindness of the blind. The certainty of the believer. The AWOL God…in an incredibly beautiful lyrical description of places and the human passion of your tormented heroes. I expect to re-read it again and again reading into new revelations and new marvels."

Walter De Hoog. Author: *Tulipano*. WWII "Resistant"

"Norman Weissman's splendid novel is a meditation on the loss of our defining ideals during war, and on the efforts of tormented souls discovering their ideologies are failed Gods. The story is driven by protagonists seeking moral redemption in a world consumed by fear, mendacity and violence. Fanatics fighting for their dogma destroy what they believe they are fighting for."

Larry Dowler   Archivist, Yale University (1970-1982)   Librarian, Widener Library, Harvard University (1982-1998)

OH PALESTINE
(The Dream Deferred)

Norman Weissman

Oh Palestine

Copyright © 2014 by Norman Weissman

All Rights reserved under International and Pan American Copyright Convention

Published in the United States by Hammonasset House Books

Mystic, CT

Cataloging-in-Publication Data is available from

Library of Congress Control Number 2007943112

History/Fiction/Middle East

ISBN 978-0-9801894-2-1

FICO: 14000

www.HammonassetHouse.com

Cover design: David Bricker

Printed in the United States of America

Oh Palestine

In Remembrance of:

Yehoshafat Harkabi

Soldier/Statesman/Teacher

(1921-1994)

Oh Palestine

PROLOGUE

This book is fiction based on fact, a record of the humanity of all who told me their stories.

Oh Palestine

"We are not passive, but active

in our own ruin;

we do not only stand under a falling house,

but pull it down upon us;

and we are not only executed,

but we are executioners,

and executioners of ourselves."

John Donne.

Oh Palestine

MITLA PASS, SINAI DESERT, JUNE 1967

One two-two-three-four! What a fucking way to fight a war! declared graffiti scrawled on a five-mile line of burned-out tanks littering Mitla Pass, a military junkyard containing the remains of an army fleeing a lost cause. A grotesque reminder of Man's ability to destroy amidst the daunting beauty of Sinai's relentless sands. Only the wind and sun now rule over a battlefield where the dead remain the unburied trash of combat. Baruch Lev, nauseated by the odor of rotting flesh, fighting the cold of a desert night, suppressed his wish to be somewhere else. Like it or not, after three wars, he had more killing to do. A duty that dry-rots the soul. Climbing to the crest of a sand dune three miles south of Mitla, Baruch Lev reconnoitered tomorrow's Body Count. There below him, bivouacked in a dry riverbed, a demoralized Egyptian battalion dug in beneath their stalled half-tracks unaware their fox holes would soon contain corpses blackened by the sun. Vultures circling overhead would soon dive down to consume the bloated remains of Fellaheen abandoned by craven Generals fleeing catastrophe.

A glowing charcoal fire provided little warmth to the Egyptians chilled by the wind. At the half-track, shouting into a microphone, the Battalion Commander's voice echoed desperation. Unable to contact anyone, he shouted a vulgar Arabic curse, turned from the half-track and walked off into the shadows leaving behind the murmured prayers of demoralized men. Clouds scudded across the sky covering the moon. Wind-driven whispering sands filled the silence of a starless night. A quiet foreboding awaited dawn as the radio's hand-cranked generator slowly ceased its agonized whine as if mourning the dead. At sunrise, Baruch Lev would feel no pride killing untrained conscripts.

The Egyptian officer walked out of the Wadi climbing the dune's steep slope. Tall, wearing a worn khaki tunic, he was a Conscript. A young University student with his first command. No professional soldier would shelter his men in a Wadi death-trap. At sunrise, attacking with machine guns and mortars, Baruch Lev's Battalion would slaughter untrained demoralized peasants fleeing destruction. For six days Israeli tanks raced ahead of the Egyptians surrounding entire Divisions. A textbook Cannae. Hannibal defeating the Romans. Lessons ignored by Generals intoxicated by the rhetoric of Islamic supremacy, fantasies dissolved by Blitzkrieg.

The Officer unbuckled his belt, pistol and holster falling to the ground. Straightening his cap, buttoning his tunic, he stepped forward, out of the dark. Young. Brave. And lost. Betrayed by incompetent leadership his men discarded weapons, abandoned fuel-starved tanks fleeing in a contagion of defeat, shedding illusions of glory and dreams of driving Israelis into the sea.

"Stop where you are," Baruch Lev shouted. The officer halted, turned to locate the voice, peering into the night from under a sweat-stained garrison cap.

"I want to surrender," the Egyptian said, stamping a boot into the sand. Shoulders back. Head high. Waiting for a reply that would be salvation. "What is your situation?" Baruch Lev asked as he approached the Egyptian. "Three days without fuel or water. Lost contact with our headquarters," he said, raising both arms in surrender. His war was over. Glad to be alive without showing the shame of defeat.

"How many are you?"

"Fifty Conscripts. Illiterate Fellaheen. Hardly able to load their guns." The Egyptian stepped forward, stamped one boot on the ground and raised his hand in a stiff military salute. A Warrior on Parade.

"Where were you going?" Baruch Lev asked. "I'm not sure," the Egyptian said. "I hope to find someone to accept our surrender."

"Do your men agree?"

"Yes."

"Will they obey orders?"

"Yes," the Egyptian said, his voice breaking. Removing his cap he nodded, saying, "All they want is to go home."

"Don't we all," Baruch Lev said, his voice softening.

"Yes, home," the Egyptian murmured, touching his forehead, lips and chest in a graceful gesture of respect. "Home sweet home." Baruch Lev holstered his pistol. "Take me to your half-track," he ordered. "Your wireless." The Officer nodded, turned, and descended into the Wadi. At the half-track he awakened a soldier. The man nodded, reached into the vehicle and removed a radio. The officer handed him a shovel. The soldier swung down, smashing the transmitter, shattering tubes, coils and wires. "Enough," Baruch Lev said. "Enough." The officer raised a hand. The soldier dropped the shovel and silently walked to the charcoal brazier. Covering his shoulders with a blanket he squatted, murmured a prayer reaching out to warm his hands over the glowing coals.

"Your compass," Baruch Lev pointed at the half-track. "Check your compass." The officer climbed into the vehicle and switched on a light. Baruch Lev removed his compass from his belt and handed it to him. "Compare yours with mine," Baruch Lev ordered. The Egyptian looked down at the dashboard. Compared the two compasses. "Madness," he shouted, "Madness! We've been retreating into Sinai." He pounded his fist on his compass as if punishing betrayal. Then, fury exhausted, his hand shaking, fighting back tears, he returned Baruch Lev's compass. "Can your men walk?" Lev asked. "Yes. We have no wounded," the officer replied. Baruch Lev handed his compass to the Egyptian. "Twenty miles west is the canal. Start before daylight. Before our planes begin strafing." The Egyptian climbed from the half-track and stiffened into a rigid brace. He stamped a boot on the sand and saluted. Baruch Lev returned the salute. With respect. "Shalom," the Egyptian said, "Shalom kind sir" he repeated, raising his hand to his cap as Baruch Lev turned, climbed the steep slope of the Wadi and walked off into the fading desert night, his departing footprints in the sand confirming the Egyptian's reprieve.

The sky darkened, clouds obscured the moon, chilled by the desert wind Baruch Lev returned to his Tank, unlaced his boots and covered himself with a blanket. He leaned back in the seat, closed his eyes and said a prayer, grateful all went well. Yes. He had done a Mitzvah. A good deed. He suppressed a laugh. A Kibbutznik who never set foot in a Synagogue did a Mitzvah? Sparing an enemy while others go on killing? Multiplying losses with an "Eye For An Eye". A hundred today. A thousand next month. A bitter harvest enabling the beast that dwells in Man to devour generations of our young without shame.

A weary voice called out of the night. "See anything Lev?"

Eyes heavy, almost closing, Baruch Lev said without emotion. "Nothing …. No one at all."

MUNICH

Of sound mind and intact body, a decorated survivor of three wars Baruch Lev said "Yes" when recruited to fight "The Long War." The one without end. Baruch Lev became enraged living a vagrant existence in barren hotel rooms exiled from the desert he loved, pursuing War Criminals hiding in raucous Beer Halls bellowing Wehrmacht marching songs, pounding "Sieg Heil! Sieg Heil!" on trembling table tops. "Sieg Heil! Sieg Heil!" They roared, arms raised, saluting Swastikas while the world trembled.

"Deutchland! Deutchland!" they sang while Rotterdam and Warsaw were reduced to rubble; "Uber Alles! Uber Alles!" they demonstrated parading under the Arc de Triumph while Paris wept. And of all the memorable Newsreel images of the past an abandoned infant, silently trembling amidst the rubble of his home could not be banished from Baruch Lev's mind wondering who that child was waiting for.

Driving from the Vier Jahreszeitin hotel on Maximillian Strasse to the airport, the shop windows along Leopold and Ungerer Strasse displaying tokens of Munich's conspicuous wealth made Baruch Lev wonder who won the War? Rising from ten million acres of rubble, Germany's Economic Miracle seemed an obscene reward for a people who forgot Slave Labor Camps crowded with Poles, Russians, and Jews. Ignored were three million survivors unable to return to their devastated homes. Out of sight were half a million DP's living behind barbed-wire in former Concentration Camps awaiting visas, or repatriation to homelands where persecution or death in a Gulag would be their fate. Forgotten were two hundred thousand kidnapped children, assigned to SS homes; blond, blue-eyed infants, future citizens of a racially pure Reich who were never reunited with their biologic parents, vanishing into the night and fog of the Third Reich where Amnesia Uber Alles closed the Gates of Memory.

For Baruch Lev, these Gates remained open. He was one who could not forget. A "Rememberer" trapped in old hopes and fears undiminished by Time. Between wars, waiting for the next to begin, he felt a constant dread, a contagion of fear with nervous tics in hand and eye identifying him as walking wounded. Only stalking and killing the enemy did he regain his one-pointed concentration on staying alive .

The Betar symbol of a raised arm brandishing a rifle inspired his teen-age years and gave his life a meaning fulfilled in wars that failed to bring lasting peace. For Baruch Lev living with fear was destiny. No longer feeling free, he tried to reclaim a mind that belonged to a State engaged in perpetual warfare.

To his neighbors, the peaceful residents of the district where Baruch Lev lived, repeated threats to his life were accepted as possible collateral damage by Terrorists. Returning to his apartment one evening his street was littered with broken glass, cordoned-off by fire engines, billows of smoke poured out of his building where twenty pounds of explosive attached to the exterior walls of his flat combined with an equal charge at the center of this force simultaneously exploded and imploded, pulverizing his home, directing deadly force to the apartment above where a nine year old girl with shattered legs became a televised political statement for the world to hear and mourn.

At the International Airport a MP checked his I.D. directing Lev to a warehouse. Baruch Lev walked to the loading ramp where an American Major sitting in a Jeep signaled with a flashlight. Baruch Lev's heart chilled, a spasm of anger tightening his gut. "Turn that damn thing off!" he ordered. The Major complied, saluted, and entered the building, his heavy footsteps pounding the concrete floor. This man's name is Trouble, Baruch Lev thought following him down a narrow aisle between rows of Cargo Containers. Reading the numbers on a Container the Major said, "Ankara. Interpol says the shipment's from Ankara." Switching on the flashlight he continued, "Another needle in a haystack, or maybe some more cold Turkey," he said, laughing at his attempt at humor. Baruch Lev remained silent thinking – where do they find these clowns? And yes. Trusting such men is stupid. And surviving stupidity goes with the mission. The Major walked into the shadows. Baruch Lev did not follow, hesitating as he heard the sound of a struggle in the darkness ahead shatter the silence. A choking sound. A gasp for breath. A death rattle. The flashlight dropped to the concrete floor. Baruch Lev turned and watched a narrow rotating light beam finger the darkness as the American staggered out of the shadows, falling forward, head down, mouth open, legs folding under him as he collapsed, both arms reaching out to Lev for support.

Baruch Lev hesitated, confused, bending over to retrieve the flashlight he felt a needle penetrate his flesh. All he saw was a thin flickering beam of light sweeping the concrete floor. And then, as the light slowly faded - darkness.

Ghosts floated around the hospital room shaving stubble on his cheeks, fluffing pillows under his neck. Baruch Lev looked up at the starched white uniform of a Nurse who failed to clear his throbbing head. He recalled the flashlight rolling across the floor and asked for the Major.

The Nurse shook her head. Looked grim. "O.D.," she said. "Nothing could be done for him. Nothing."

He did not understand. Asked again.

"Overdose," she said. "The Major's gone. It's a miracle you're alive." She floated from the room bearing a tray of medications leaving behind confusion, fear, and a lingering antiseptic odor. Yes. De-toxification takes time. So, patience. Wait for a clear mind to think with. Yes. Yes. Remember that futile mission if that helps. Or better, think about all you love far away. Far, far away.

Baruch Lev thought about the desert, an endless ocean of sand flowing under a blue cloudless sky and shimmering heat-haze horizons. At night, an infinite dome of stars transited an indifferent Universe. His spiritual home, the eternal desert. Free of the stink and horror of cities where desperate humans fight for a place to live. The desert contained no distractions, no refuge hiding a man from himself. The desert magnified everything. An arena worthy of a man's soul where Truth could not be evaded. Where agonies clarified. Exposed to burning winds, bone chilling nights, in the desert Baruch Lev found his vision of God. In the desert he felt invulnerable. Absorbed in the stars. The magnetic streams and oceans of the sky were his companions in the watchtowers of his fortress home and farm. He passionately studied the night sky, the unchanging Universe held his attention until at the first explosive whine of a Sniper's bullet he crouched behind a thick protective shield of steel, a field telephone ringing, anxious voices bringing him back to that barren speck of desert he was prepared to die for. "All's well!" he answered, cranking the telephone's generator. "All's well! All's Well!" he shouted. Then gratefully he returned to his Talmud, his Torah, his Testament – the stars. Always the stars.

And yes, indeed, Baruch Lev's fate was not in his stars – but in himself. Away from his beloved desert, he endured the treachery of cities and bureaucratic stupidity that offended his spirit. He learned violence is the language nations speak bulldozing homes without considering where the homeless would live. And when driven by fanatical faith Allah Akbar attacked his people they became what they opposed, injuring what they saved, a nation concealing despair with Rules of Engagement, sanitizing genocide as Surgical Strikes. This tall, handsome Kibbutznik, irrigated the desert and fought three wars before becoming a hero who betrayed his past, serving his idea of Justice until he learned Justice is for God alone to decide.

KIBBUTZ YAD MORDECHAI

He was one year old when Aaron, his father, felt his arms, thumped his chest, and looked into his eyes. "This one will never make a farmer," he said, turning to friends crowding the Kibbutz nursery. "The arms are too short, and see, the back is not put together in the right way. He is no farmer." His mother laughed. "Our son will be a teacher. See how big his head is. That is to fill with learning and teach others." A crowd of eager parents glanced at the clock as they visited their children separated all day from their homes. In forty minutes family-time ended, and with hugs, kisses and tears parents returned to their livestock and orange groves delegating the nurturing of children to experts. At sixteen, Baruch Lev fulfilled his mother's prophecy. A large head on a short, thin body soon held all the Kibbutz schoolmaster could teach. He was accepted at the University. "A great honor," Aaron said, embracing his son, proud of an achievement that brought honor to the family and a joy that made his aged and weathered face young. "Yes, Papa," Baruch Lev replied, hesitating, unaccustomed to praise. "An honor you earned," said Aaron becoming more effusive. Sending a student from the Kibbutz to be educated was a great distinction. One that was not unknown, for their family was descended from learned Talmudists who believed study was a sacred act.

"You will not find people so different in the city. Be not afraid," Aaron said, his wrinkled khaki shorts and sweat-stained shirt clinging to his thick arms and legs. "I am nervous Papa," Baruch Lev said.

"Yes. Prudence is wise. Fear poison." Aaron held up gnarled work-stained hands. "In the old days all we had was our hands. No horse. No mule. Like animals we pulled plows. You forget working like a slave when you have a dream. There is no time for worry when all you think about is the future. The end of misery." He wiped his forehead with a faded canvas hat looking like a Chagall painting of a Patriarch. "We were brave. Fearing no one. I always knew when there was danger. Did you know that?"

"No Papa."

Aaron pressed a hand over his heart as if taking an oath. "They said it was God's Will and I said why should he protect someone like me? Then they said I must be under the protection of the Devil and I said it was only my nose. A Man who does not use tobacco can smell an Arab mile away!"

Baruch Lev shook his head and laughed.

"Neither God or the Devil saved me! Do you understand? I learned how to think for myself so that others would never do my thinking for me." His voice softened. "Never listened to the Big-shots visiting our Kibbutz in their fancy motor cars. Our war heroes with Torah in one hand, a gun in the other. Never! Never! Believe me, you can die from such men!" Aaron swayed back and forth searching for words, evoking buried feelings. "Trust what you truly believe and you will avoid killing men no better or worse than yourself. Do you understand?"

"I think so Papa."

"I have seen a lifetime of killing and done my share. I pray you will be spared that horror. Killing poisons your life."

"Yes Papa."

"Once I believed in killing men who made Pogroms. I burned villages killing women and children and now I fear killing will never end. Like a raging fever killing paralyzes our mind, destroying all restraint. Makes us unfeeling. Without humanity. And when the dead come alive in our quiet moments, or in our dreams, we know we have lost something vital we will never regain. A quiet conscience. Killing can never redeem men who fight to hold on to what they believe was given them by God."

"You doubt Torah, Papa?"

"Yes. And so must you. Question everything. For that is how you become your own man. Free. Honorable. Without shame. Or remorse. Understand?"

"I think I do, Papa. I think I do."

As the Galilee Hills emerged from shadows slowly dissolving in the early light of dawn, Baruch Lev drove through fertile acres salvaged from forbidding malarial swamps. Draining marshland eradicated fevers, making the region habitable for Arab and Jew. Today sugar beets, cotton, peanuts and citrus groves perfumed the air. One afternoon, driving through this region with his son, exhilarated by the sight of a lush harvest, Aaron shouted: "A Hell-hole! A God-forsaken swamp! When we purchased this wasteland not even an Arab would live here. Now Look! Look!" He pounded the door with his fist, shaking his head in joy and wonder. Then silent he descended into reverie, staring out the window. "Unbelievable," he murmured. "Incredible," he said, recalling years plowing his youth and strength into this once barren soil. "We did the dirty work. Everything! We were never fancy intellectuals doing nothing but talk! We did the hard work," Aaron said, "and now all I ask," he continued, plaintive, repeating a recurring request "is a little visit now and then."

Regular visits were infrequent. Tomorrow Baruch Lev returned to Munich. Perhaps to never see Aaron alive again.

During 1917's Influenza winter, Aaron closed his East End London shop and enlisted in a dream. Assigning his inventory of second-hand furniture to unhappy creditors, he joined the British Army's Jewish Brigade. Between Zionism and bankruptcy he did not hesitate. He opted for the hot desert sun, Mediterranean beaches, and a vision of lush orange groves. Any war, anywhere, would be better than fighting in France's blood-soaked trenches. In November he marched into Jerusalem with General Allenby. The Ottoman Empire, defeated on the Damascus Plains, abandoned their Middle East provinces. Aaron learned discipline, saw the transformation of untrained men by a good scrub-up, clean uniforms, and a correct parade. If this made an Empire then other men, even Ghetto Jews acquiring these skills could build a nation. Perhaps Zionism was not an impossible dream?

Aaron welcomed his son from the doorway of a small, white-washed cinder-block house. They embraced and entered a room furnished with a table, electric hot plate, and a bed. Aaron went to the kitchen filling a tea kettle under a water tap that gurgled and spat as it purged air. Ten years a widower, Aaron retained an old soldier's self-sufficiency. Pressed shirts. Immaculate Quarters. Rigid self-discipline. "Fifty years a farmer, a Mujik," Aaron boasted. "Now all I do is lounge around in drip-dry pajamas and read." Aaron poured and steeped the tea as he waited for a reply. "Let's take a walk," Aaron said. "Meet some of our young widows. Believe me, we have some selection. Great beauties." With a sweep of his hand he carved the air, describing a buxom figure. Baruch Lev went to the sink ignoring the suggestion. Staring into a mirror he washed his hands, thinking, Yes, The Old Man hasn't changed. And what's more he looks younger than I do. Aaron sipped tea holding a sugar cube between his teeth, staring at his son. "So, tell me, how are the heroes? Our Generals?" He poured a second cup, added milk, the kettle whistling as he placed it on the electric burner. "Generals are a disaster as politicians when they win elections to justify their bloody wars." Aaron paused. Another sip. "Like Marshal Petain, hero of Verdun and what he did to France." Baruch Lev remained silent. Silence had become the language they spoke when visiting. Aaron insisted. "You should read about Petain. Then you'll understand how heroes devour our young. Three thousand this year. A thousand next. A hundred here, three hundred there! A gross national income in flesh and blood!"

Baruch Lev turned and stared out the window thinking – leave before dark? Another hour, maybe?

"So, you have orders?" Aaron asked, refilling both cups.

"Yes."

"Europe?"

"Yes."

"Mister nobody. Nowhere. No Poppa. No Mama. No frying pan." He repeated the taunting refrain without a smile.

"It's what I do."

"You look like a cadaver. I want to see grandchildren before I die. What you need is a home and a wife. Not more hotel rooms."

"My work is important."

Aaron set the tea kettle on the burner. "What's so important? Your life's not important I suppose?"

"Let's go for a walk."

"No more talking?"

"Yes, Poppa. No more. Please."

"Then why visit? Why come if we don't talk? If nothing personal or human or with feeling is discussed? What in God's name are you? A Golem risking your life for fanatics preaching their Greater Israel fantasy. Acquiring land instead of wisdom. Hating Arabs more than they love their children. Brutalized young soldiers shooting rubber-coated bullets at Arab kids throwing stones and fire-bombs in the name of Allah. If you ask me we will die from this lunacy destroying the land of our dreams. Good old Israel. We didn't come here to be persecutors and victimizers of others, isolated from the world, ruled by the Synagogue and not the State. Religious extremism was never our purpose. Freedom. Justice. Peace for all was what we fought and died for. Fanaticism will destroy by the sword all who live by the sword! And we cannot save ourselves dancing under the wedding canopy with Arab negotiators with no intention of making a marriage. Sooner or later the bride's family will discover they're being had."

"The government's doing everything possible," Lev replied.

"You are not Superman and the decay rate of hate is zero. When the myth of our invincibility is sacred, when we sacrifice every human value in the name of national security what remains? Who are we? What have we become?"

"Little David confronting Goliath."

"Tell me my son, who do you think is Goliath?"

MUNICH

On a cobble-stoned street off Josephsplatz, Sanctuary, a crowded smoke-filled Café welcomed avid newspaper readers and homeless Drifters drinking coffee and eating pastries. Noted for discreet waiters and unhurried customers, without the raucous table-pounding of a Bauhaus, undocumented foreign workers and the stateless enjoyed political asylum where the Police were not too diligent enforcing immigration Laws. Photographs on the walls memorialized Munich's Golden Age celebrating artists, actors, authors and musicians who in 1933 disappeared. Vanished forever were a generation of intellectuals who nourished the hearts and minds of Europe's most civilized nation. A bookcase on the rear wall displayed a row of distinguished books and a sign:

BURNED IN 1933 (by order of the SS)

reminding Baruch Lev of Heinrich Heine's prescient warning: "a nation that burns books will soon burn people."

On other walls were photographs of University students with dueling-scarred faces certifying initiation into Aryan manhood unaware they were destined for a frozen death on Russia's endless Steppes. A doomed generation, progeny of a nation intoxicated by dreams of conquest. Exposed to incessant propaganda they became Hitler's Ubermench, fanatical purifiers of the sacred Germanic bloodstream led by Generals seeking personal glory in genocidal warfare, exchanging honor and personal integrity for Field Marshal's Batons and, at their throats, Iron Crosses with diamond clusters.

There were no decorations with diamonds on the British Army's Jewish Brigade's uniforms. A Star of David worn on a shoulder patch identified Baruch Lev as an Israeli entering a concentration camp where emaciated survivors with haggard faces stumbled and crawled through the barbed wire rising to their feet to welcome him. The strongest emerged from the surging crowd reaching out in their first triumphant moment of freedom to touch and lovingly caress his Star of David. Dismayed by the overwhelming horror greeting him, overcome by his feelings, Lev walked among the starving prisoners unable to reach out and embrace them. Confused. Not knowing what to do, he put down his weapon, turned away from the survivors and sobbed. Then, after a moment of silence, accompanied by the pounding of his heart, slowly, almost inaudibly, as if in a far away miraculous resurrection, a thousand trembling voices cried out and chanted in a fervent chorus rising to a roar of celebration – a mournful prayer of exultation: "Shema Yisrael, Adonai Eluhainu, Adonai Echod! – Hear, O Israel: The Lord is our God, the Lord is One!"

Yes. The past is never past, it is always with us Baruch Lev thought, remembering the day they were ordered to take revenge; a consuming rage turned decent men into assassins stalking Europe for War Criminals. They became avid hunters identifying murderers by name, rank, and serial numbers; daunting faces with triumphant smiles revealing with what consummate joy otherwise ordinary citizens kill.

Baruch Lev's first War Criminal was tall, retaining the straight-back long-legged stride of the Waffen SS as he walked out of a crowded Bauhaus after an evening of dark beer, raucous songs and table pounding. A dueling scar on one cheek and a pinned-up sleeve where once there was an arm confirmed the positive identification permitting Baruch Lev to kill.

Christmas 1945. In a village of snow-covered roofs in an isolated Alpine valley, holiday candles decorating windows welcomed visitors with traditional Bavarian charm.

Across the street from a festive Bauhaus, waiting in a darkened doorway, Baruch Lev watched spirals of wood smoke rising into the clear cold night. Listening to laughter and loud singing reminded Lev of other joyous celebrations. Far away. In another lifetime. Yes indeed. Christmas Eve was not a good night to seek justice. He stepped from the shadows following his Quarry, their footsteps muffled in ankle-deep snow. Without breaking stride the SS Officer turned and walked into a passageway between two houses. Baruch Lev watched him walk to the end of the alley where opening his heavy winter overcoat he spread his legs and urinated. Baruch Lev waited a moment and then asked: "Standartenfuhrer?"

The SS man laughed and nodded. His bladder drained, he buttoned his overcoat, turned and slowly walked back to the street.

"Standartenfuhrer?" Baruch Lev asked again. "Ja!" the man said, raising one arm in a Nazi Party greeting.

Baruch Lev waited at the end of the alley as the SS man approached. A silent night. A still night, footsteps muffled in the fallen snow.

"Ja! Ja! Ich bin ein Standartenfuhrer."

"I bring you greetings," Baruch Lev said.

"Greetings?"

"From your friends in Tel Aviv."

"I have no friends in Tel Aviv," the SS Officer said, his mind clearing as he turned and fled to the end of the passageway where a single silenced shot staggered him, stumbling a few steps before falling face down in the snow.

Baruch Lev waited a moment before entering the alley. Fired again, serving what he believed was Justice.

Justice? There was no Justice on May 14th 1948 when five Arab Armies attempted to drive Baruch Lev off his land. Surrounded by Egyptians for three days, his Kibbutz sheltered women and children in underground Bunkers before evacuating them to safety; the mothers remained to feed their men, load guns, and fight. Determined their children will not be scattered by the winds of war to perish in the desert sands of their Promised Land, they loaded them on an Army truck with food and water and a small suitcase of warm clothing. Baruch Lev prayed that God would protect the innocent. But neither God nor Justice prevailed that day when a roadside mine detonated. There were no survivors.

Awakening, watching shadows on the walls, grotesque shapes choreographed by sunlight streaming through the window, Baruch Lev believed another day in Munich would be one day too many. Shoving aside bed covers, stretching and yawning, he waited a moment to clear sleep from his eyes. He did not think he could survive another year of futile stake-outs tracking informants who earned their wages selling deceit. He wanted to go home to whatever he could rebuild from the fragments of his life. And that, he recognized in a moment of candid self-recognition, was not to be. He would salute and follow orders though reluctant to serve in the needless wars of old Generals sending young men to die. He had trained to fight and kill. Now after twenty years, he discovered he wanted to retrieve what he had given to the State. A life he could call his own. This awareness was troubling. At the bathroom mirror he studied his unshaven face saddened to find sorrowful eyes, lips pressed together in a thin line of bitterness telling him no one lives forever. Sooner or later he will be terminated. Lathering with shaving soap, acquiring a creamy white beard, his razor uncovered a suntan that made him look youthful, more resolute. Though he no longer was emboldened with a warrior's feeling of overwhelming power enabling soldiers to kill with impunity, the distinction between combatants and civilians seemed blurred. Had he become a War Criminal?

What would he say in his defense if there was a trial? What could he say to justify wars defending a homeland that despite 20 thousand dead never became secure? He was protecting a nation living in fear. Anxious citizens convinced it could happen again. If there was a trial certainly the Court would recognize the more wars they fought for the right to live in peace the more elusive that goal became. No fair-minded Judge could condemn a people for whom war and peace alternated in an insane dance of death with each generation bringing forth other Isaacs to be sacrificed to whatever Gods there may be. Yes. His people had a right to do whatever was necessary to defend themselves. If we are to live by the sword, let us see that it is kept strong in the hand, rather than at our throat.

Baruch Lev was native born, a Sabra. A desert fruit. Hard on the outside with a tender inner core. A person of contradictions. Lawless and law abiding, compassionate and cruel, determined to never be a hapless victim marching off to a gas chamber driven from his home. History made Sabras relentless, with one immutable message to the world: "Never again. Never!"

He inherited his father's fears despite what they achieved making the desert fertile, creating a homeland, fighting wars, burying twenty thousand dead while enduring the threat of annihilation.

"The sins of the fathers shall not be inherited by the sons," the Talmud says. Yet when sons commit sins of their own, if what they do to survive corrupts what they are fighting for, can they stay sane? Can they see themselves as the world sees them? Are they leading a nation to self-destruction?

The Freedom Fighters were entering the Palestinian camp to drive out terrorists, said the Christian Phalange Militia entering Chatila's southern gate during the first Lebanon war. Without orders to stop them, Baruch Lev's Tanks surrounded the camp, illuminating the slaughter with flares. When they entered the camp after three days the dead were everywhere. Women, young men, babies, grandparents, machine-gunned to death. Young men and boys shot in the back of the head in ritual executions. Hospital patients castrated, butchered in their beds. Piles of corpses, arms and legs entangled in grotesque mounds of flesh and blood covered by clouds of flies. The Israeli Generals were accomplices to genocide by their Phalangist Allies.

"Israelis don't do that sort of thing," the government spokesman explained. "It was the Christians," he said, as if blaming the Phalangists mitigated shame, for shame is corrosive. Like water dripping on stone, shame penetrates deep into the soul compelling Baruch Lev to speak out against another war of choice. For saying "No" to more incursions and atrocities he received six months confinement without pay. His crime: "Insubordination and behavior prejudicial to good order and discipline".

ACRE FORTRESS PRISON

High on a graffiti-covered wall of a narrow prison cell in the Acre Fortress, a barred window brought in the summer's hot desert winds and the winter's chill. A hard sleeping pad on a cold stone floor, a small sink, an open squat toilet with a dim light bulb flickering overhead furnished what the Army considered proper solitary confinement. For six months Baruch Lev received two servings of unappetizing food a day. Enough to keep him alive. To feed his mind the names, dates, and messages on the walls provided his library of hope; despairing voices read with humility. What would he someday write? What words would he leave behind enabling other prisoners to understand his offense? To resist the murder of his soul he disobeyed an unlawful order. Unable to share his country's hysteria made him an outlaw where dissent was treason. A betrayal of what he once was willing to die for. His Prosecutors insisted: "War is Hell. Casualties the price of freedom. We do what we must do to survive." Lev would one day write his reply on the walls proclaiming to all future occupants - there is another way. A way that does not betray our past to protect our future. A way that does not repeat years of bloodshed with unchanged results. A way that does not corrupt our young by intensifying their hatreds, demonizing the enemy. A way that does not destroy the future by ignoring the humane values of our past. Now, before it is too late, we must question what kind of nation will survive if we win?

Thoughts compelling Baruch Lev to recall a friend he could never forget. Rajoub, a man defined by what he fought for. An Arab who worked beside Baruch Lev harvesting Pecans as they talked and sang together in the hot mid-day sun, an enduring friendship contradicting the belief the only good Arab is a dead Arab. "You can't build a democracy on a foundation of theft, fear and illegality," Rajoub said, breaking their agreed silence about politics. "If you prick us do we not bleed?" Rajoub continued, taunting his old friend. "If you tickle us, do we not laugh?" he asked, "If you poison us, do we not die? And if you wrong us? Shall we not revenge?"

Baruch Lev bent over to fill his basket, ignoring his friend's taunting quotations.

"Who do you think we are," Rajoub said, rising from his knees. Standing erect, holding up a basket of Pecans like a Priest sanctifying The Host. "Are we not Brothers? Children of Abraham and Sarah and Hagar? Do we not have eyes, hands, organs, dimensions, senses, affections, passions? What do you think we feel when you take our land and water, bulldoze our homes, kill our children, destroy our villages, burn our cities, assassinate our leaders, withhold our food and goods, making our lives miserable with walls and checkpoints and bureaucratic harassments? What do you think we feel?"

Baruch Lev put down his basket. He turned to Rajoub and said. "What do you think we feel huddled in bomb shelters? What are your fanatics teaching us when we are unable to walk our streets, eat in a restaurant, ride our Buses, send our children to school in the morning not knowing if they will live through the day? What lessons have we learned when your mad men drive us crazy with fear?" Rajoub waited a moment, hesitating to discuss the undeniable truths of the life they shared. "And what do you think we have learned when you fight your bloody wars, destroying our homes, our lands? When you kill us with impunity you destroy not only our lives, but also our humanity."

The two men, Arab and Jew, returned to work harvesting, bending down to the ground, filling their baskets with pecans.

"Insha'Allah," Baruch Lev said, breaking the silence. God's Will! he said his voice grieving. "is salaam alaykum." May peace be with you!

Sharing his friend's sorrow Rajoub replied - "Allahu Akbar, God is great! wa alaykum is salaam. With you be peace!"

Baruch Lev also recalled Rajoub kneeling to pray, unrolling his rug on the ground, his haunting voice rising in a joy that evoked the religiosity of his childhood reminding him of what he had lost. Gone forever were conversations with God, believing in his protection, with the All Mighty not so All Mighty anymore. With a normal life denied to both Arab and Jew, Baruch Lev wondered - what are we fighting for as we march arm in arm into the long dark night of our despair?

In a prison cell, with his mind evoking vivid images, Baruch Lev occupied a land of mystery called the past. His days and nights were alive with memories that evoked remorse. No face or name was beyond recall. He felt exiled from the people he loved remembering all the hard choices of his life, the lives destroyed, the villages razed. He learned he could see the stars only when it is dark, defeating loneliness by learning one experiences little but oneself. Solitude became a mirror enabling him to revisit his life. Refusing to choose between love of country and love of justice, Baruch Lev felt like a ghost among lost men.

Tedious hours searching for Informers selling misinformation yielded little intelligence. A fool's game not worth the time, money and lives lost for the illusion of being well-informed. Bad food and sleepless nights in barren hotel rooms depressed the Hunter who knew he is also hunted. He recalled the Sanctuary Café where drug dealers and informants gathered to read newspapers while at adjacent tables obese patrons with spotless white napkins tucked under bulging chins ate prodigiously. Pipe and cigar addicts clouding the room with smoke sipped coffee and nibbled Strudel. At other tables lovers held hands and embraced, making Baruch Lev wonder how long it has been since he had been with a woman. He stirred sugar and cream in his cup raising it to his lips as he remembered a lover who was no more, a casualty of war. She brewed his morning coffee, cooked his meals, and shared his bed so much a part of him the two often seemed one flesh. Living alone, watching others embrace, their tender feelings reminded him of what he missed; a touch, a caress, passion aroused by a warm body trembling in his arms. A waiter interrupted his reverie, filling his cup as he ordered food and opened a book reading to ignore the laughter around him. He wanted to escape a mind unable to erase memory of the betrayed Zionist dream. A nation built by survivors who endured hunger and fear and the world's indifference; heroic men and women overcoming despair, dying in wars of liberation, becoming hated occupiers who learned, after 20 thousand dead, life becomes hideous when they surrender to hatred.

Now separated from the people he loved he felt like a Pariah. He put down the book and closed his eyes to escape his thoughts. He knew he could no longer continue searching for faces and names and ten thousand SS numbers tattooed under arms; wandering from city to city, airport to airport, hotel to hotel in a merry-go-round of pursuit and murder for that was what he had become, sanctified and blessed and licensed by a higher authority, not for vengeance but in the undeniable existential need for survival. Questioning what survived was his crime. He nodded at the waiter who refilled his cup. Baruch Lev leaned back in his chair, closed his eyes and saw mercy and justice give way to xenophobia and a failure to fulfill the promise of Abraham.

Oh Palestine

"Never say all is hopeless

life is through

when clouds of darkness

hide skies of blue.

The day we are waiting for is coming

Yes it's near.

The world will hear our footsteps

Will know we are here."

Hirsch Glick

Vilna Ghetto

Age 16

DACHAU CONCENTRATION CAMP

Tourists visiting Germany's Death Camps pose for souvenir photographs at the Crematoria or beneath a Gallows dangling a Hangman's Noose. Genocide is now rarely talked about when not actively denied. A sign above the entrance gate, Arbeit Macht Frei proclaimed the cruel promise of SS Guards escorting Jews on their journey to oblivion, evoking laughter when Beer Steins were raised at the end of the workday supervising Hitler's killing machine. For victims, Work Makes You Free was a hope soon vanished up the chimneys.

At the far wall of the camp, a narrow bridge crossed a moat enclosing a separate compound containing a gallows, gas chamber, crematoria and mounds of ashes marked by Stars of David or Crosses. Baruch Lev walked the gravel footpath past signs in five languages citing numbers, nationalities, and religions of the dead. He turned to watch an old man and woman in blue coveralls raking the grounds. Not a stray leaf, candy wrapper, or a discarded cigarette desecrated the site. Stabbing spiked sticks into the ground to pick up the litter, they worked bent-over, heads bowed as if praying at a shrine.

Inside the Museum photographs documented the assembly, transportation and extermination of victims whose hair, teeth and shoes were hoarded with miserly passion. Meticulous records noted children under five transported free, half-fare for those under ten, and for groups of over four hundred, generous excursion rates were available. A bargain meticulously recorded in newsreel films of distraught parents and terrified children carrying suitcases and backpacks, pushing overloaded prams from every European city embarking on an unimaginable Exodus escorted by young German soldiers aiming rifles at children.

Returning to Munich Baruch Lev drove past a young woman standing on the side of the road with her thumb raised. He stopped and leaned across the seat to unlock the car door. "Munich" the Hitch-hiker asked, her upturned face framed in a parka hood. Baruch Lev nodded as she slid into the seat and pulled back the hood revealing a classic profile.

"Been to Dachau?" he asked, turning to look at her.

"Oh yes," she said. Nodding. Trembling from the cold, her lips pressed together. Baruch Lev recalled seeing her standing in front of a photograph covering an entire wall next to the exit. She stared at the photomural, as if overwhelmed, crying, ignoring visitors forced to walk around her as they exited the museum's grim interior into bright Bavarian sunshine. Impatient, most Tourists hurried past the photograph, heads turned from the haunting image of two emaciated young girls embracing in mutual protection and love, their eyes bright with the exultation of survivors, faces scrubbed clean, hair brushed and combed, two resurrected lives smiling at the camera.

The Hitch-hiker warmed her hands over the car's hot air duct. Baruch Lev turned and studied her face reddened by the cold. She looked familiar.

"There's a Café ahead," he said. "Coffee?"

"Oh yes." She said as Baruch Lev turned off the highway and parked at a Roadhouse with a Stork's Roost on the roof and a large picture window in the front wall. They sat at a table where she draped her parka over the back of a chair. Then she turned to him and said: "So you are not an American?"

"Israeli."

"That explains your accent," she said with a disarming smile. " I like how you speak German."

"Danke."

Baruch Lev nodded to the waiter. Cake appeared on the table. The Hitch-hiker made a wry face. Her head shaking. "To hell with my figure," she said without embarrassment as her fork carved and raised a large slice to her mouth.

Baruch laughed. "A Fashion Model?" he asked.

"How did you know?"

"Models either eat like Sparrows or stuff their faces."

She turned and grinned. Her mouth full. "I was once very beautiful," she said, leaning back in her chair, surveying the room, staring at adjacent tables. Still beautiful, Baruch Lev thought. A Nordic or Slavic beauty. High cheekbones. A Fashion photographers dream. "I don't belong here," she said, gesturing with her thumb, turning to the other diners. "With them." She nodded at the well-fed patrons crowding the café.

"What brings you to Munich?" she asked.

"Citrus. I export Citrus."

"That explains why you are here," she said. "You have no choice."

" I go where they send me. A Commercial Traveler."

" I understand. For me it is different." Staring at the other Patrons, her expression objected to the raucous laughter, the arrogant voices. "Germany!" she said, waving an imaginary flag like a Patriot at a parade. "Welcome to the New Reich."

"Why don't you emigrate?"

She remained silent a moment. Troubled. Ruefully shaking her head. Turning to face Lev. "We are all responsible for the Nazi Jack-boots, the book burnings, Dachau. Bergen Belsen. Treblinka. Aushwitz. You have a past to be proud of. What can Germans boast of? BMW's? Color TV's? Refrigerators? Prosperity Uber Alles?" Baruch Lev stirred his coffee without replying. "Our Universities were corrupted," she explained. "What can we learn from Professors who conceal our shame?" Her voice filled the room. Heads turned. Listening. "We knew right from wrong!" she shouted. "Knew the difference between Thomas Mann and Heinrich Himmler! We were taught silence. Complicity. Deny the SS uniform in Daddy's closet." Her shrill voice evoked anger at an adjacent table. "Communist Bitch!" a red-faced apoplectic man shouted. Another cried "Red Whore!" Baruch Lev signaled the waiter for the bill, tipping generously. Other Patrons muttered insults. The Hitch-Hiker refused to hurry. Forked another slice of cake into her mouth deliberately drinking her coffee slowly before exiting the room head high, ignoring the hostile crowd.

Driving to Munich they listened to music. Fine-tuned the radio, adjusted the volume.

"That I like," she said. "I like Brahms."

Baruch Lev welcomed her changed mood. He disliked being conspicuous. The road ahead darkened. He turned the headlights on.

"Dachau can be depressing," he said.

"Why do you go?" she asked, turning to him.

He hesitated. Nodded. "To understand," he explained" A good reason," she said. "Logical. Intelligent."

"I know," he said.

What else makes sense? Survivor Guilt? You are alive. Six million are not."

Baruch Lev waited a moment. "That's possible," he said.

"Can there be another reason?"

"Respect for the dead. To remember. And other reasons beyond understanding."

"I only know it can happen again. It is happening again." She stared out the window her mood set for a spell of riot.

"The Bitch that bore him is in heat again," Baruch Lev said.

Surprised. Shaking her head she turned and asked: 'You know Brecht?"

"A few lines."

"Then get the words right," she insisted, her voice rising." Don't yet rejoice in his defeat you men…although the world stood up and stopped the Bastard…the Bitch that bore him is in heat again."

"Yes. It is a Bitch-filled world," Baruch Lev replied, startled by her anger as she said: "If only we could act instead of talking."

"More Brecht" Baruch Lev asked.

"Yes. He had the words. Spoke the truth. We see the horror. Become accomplices. Go on with our lives blind to evil. We remained silent as they build crematoriums. The gas ovens will burn again."

Staring out the window they listened to the music. Then the news. Trivia. Tragedy. Government statements announced with equal emphasis. Another hi-jacking. A soccer team defeated. Terrorist bombings in Beirut, Belfast, Buenos Aires. "Germany has abolished memory," she said. "We have amputated our history. We have no feeling for our armies lost in Russia. Millions dead who disappear unless we remember them. Only money and new cars concern us. Lose an arm, a leg, you feel pain, our body does not forget a missing limb. An entire nation amputates twelve years and remembers nothing."

In Munich neon-lit shop windows displayed the latest Paris fashions. Pedestrians dutifully waited at intersections for signal lights to change. "Good obedient Germans," the Hitch-hiker said, opening the door, glancing at the crowded side-walk with a disdainful smile. "Danke," she said, stepping on to the curb, merging with the crowd, disappearing around the corner. Baruch Lev leaned across the seat and locked the door. The light turned green. Then he realized he never asked her name. "Auf wiedersehn," Baruch Lev said, to no one but himself as he drove off into the night wondering where he had seen that beautiful face before?

MARIENDORF DISPLACED PERSONS CAMP

Her name was Inga Spandau, born in a crowded Bunker under Berlin's smoldering rubble, her first breath tasted of burnt cordite and the odor of putrefying flesh. A bastard Russenkinder, conceived in an orgy of rape by Russian soldiers, Inga was a bitter harvest on a continent seeded by several million corpses. Weaned on suffering, stained by her cruel paternity, Air Raid sirens and explosions were childhood's most vivid memories. In May 1945, when the chattering guns ceased their frightening dirge, Inga and her mother Sybille crawled out of the rubble into the verdant beauty of a now silent Spring that mocked their misery. In devastated Dresden, Hamburg, Cologne and Berlin, life slowly resurrected in the ruins. From the Vistula to the Rhine, from the Baltic to the Danube, bomb-shocked survivors emerged from cellars to chalk family names on signposts, unaware ten years would elapse before being reunited with their fathers, sons and husbands returning from Russian POW camps. During The Hunger Years, Sybille joined other Hausfraus clearing rubble for a bowl of soup from Russian Army Field Kitchens. Twenty thousand women unaided by their humiliated men, swept Germany's streets. Indomitable Hausfraus cleaned up the catastrophe wrought by futile dreams of conquest. When American G.I.'s occupied their sector, the Spandaus revived on Spam and powdered eggs. Brutal Russian gang-rape gave way to American K-rations, chewing gum, cigarettes and chocolate bars. Living under the protection of a G.I. was welcomed by Occupation Wives to survive the hunger and cold of a winter without fuel.

Inga Spandau recalled a shy gum-chewing G.I., speaking comic book German bringing rucksacks of food every night. The passionate moans of Sybille and her lover behind the blanket wall dividing their flat aroused Inga Spandau's first erotic fantasies. Sex, she learned was as life-sustaining as food. When the soldier returned to America, Sybille found another G.I. until they were relocated to the Mariendorf Displaced Persons Camp.

Housed behind barbed wire in a former concentration camp the Spandaus joined liberated Polish and Russian Slave Laborers, displaced Germans, orphaned children and death camp survivors waiting for foreign Visas. Leaders proclaiming the Four Freedoms during the war now were indifferent to their fate. At Mariendorf fifty thousand DP's laughed, cried, argued, made love, married and birthed babies, their days and nights filled with a Babel of languages lamenting their stateless agony. Each ethnic group clustered together by nationality defended their own living space. Watching the hopeless lay down on their bunks and turn their faces to the wall and die taught Inga Spandau death was not a reasonable choice. She determined to accept suffering and not flee into a meaningless death choosing to live and endure life in all its terrors.

After morning Role Call, to escape feeling imprisoned inside barbed wire, Inga Spandau sought freedom hiding in a corner of a small wooden tool shed. Alone in the dark she evoked thoughts, memories, and dreams sustaining her desire to live, imagining a childhood she never had, a life with a home, a father, a family. She often wondered who was her father? Did he survive the war? Would she ever find and confront him with his crime, her existence? Yes, she vowed, I will not be like other DP's trapped in despair. I will live a life worth living. Do more than survive. I will become someone who changes the world. I will travel. I will work. And then I will love and be loved in return. No longer a victim I will become my destiny. A weapon. An arrow on a tightly drawn bow that when released will make history.

Despairing, her mother Sybille did not share Inga's vows retaining only bitter memories. And when She broke down and surrendered to sorrow, Inga held her mother in her arms as she would a child. "We must never cease fighting for our place in the world," Inga insisted as Sybille pulled away from her daughter's embrace, shaking her head angrily. "There will be no place for us anymore," Sybille said. "There will be no place on earth where Germans will be welcome." Inga embraced her mother and began brushing her hair, long rhythmic strokes to restore calm. "Be grateful we are alive," Inga pleaded. Sybille pushed Inga aside refusing to be comforted. "Germany has forfeited the respect of our neighbors," Sybille said. "For twelve years we were consumed by our hatreds and now will be hated forever." Inga remained silent. Fighting back tears. Hopeless, Sybille recalled: "We were not always like this. Defeated. Defenseless. Ashamed. Sybille rose to her feet and stepped to the window, looking off into the distance, recalling the past. "I remember Germany before the crooked cross replaced the Crucifix, before Hitler with his sly magic poured his poison into us, before parents allowed children to go goose-stepping off to war, before marriage vows were desecrated by the State, where bondage of an entire nation replaced the holy bonds of family and church, parent and child, brother and sister. I remember a Germany that led the world in science, in culture, in music, in art. I remember a Germany where men had courage and honor and defended their families from a government that corrupted our souls. I remember a Germany that is no more and will never be again."

Inga, moved by her mother's despair, remained silent. Sybille's recollections forged in Inga a fierce determination to repair the world. There must be a better way, she thought. Bringing people together, banishing hunger and poverty. But first the past must be destroyed.

Within the deepest recesses of her being she found strength conceived in the violence of her creation, the agony of her birth, the privations of the war, the misery of the DP camp. Yes. If necessary to make a better world, I will kill or be killed.

Waiting at the camp gate for the daily Transports to arrive, Joseph, a ten year old boy obsessed by his memories, compared the new faces with images from his past. As the DP's carrying battered suitcases and torn rucksacks disembarked from the trucks, Joseph carefully studied them. Closing his eyes and shaking his head, he endured each day's bitter disappointment without complaint.

In 1939, when the SS selected his family for resettlement Joseph was rescued from a Death Train by a courageous Polish woman who knew his family. During the Occupation 200,000 blond blue-eyed infants were kidnapped from Dutch, Polish and Ukrainian homes for adoption by barren SS couples to meet the Thousand Year Reich's need for racially pure citizens. Born a Jew, raised a Catholic, blond blue-eyed Joseph was taken from his Polish rescuer, vanishing into the Night and Fog of German occupied Europe. In 1945, liberated from his SS family by the Americans, Joseph relocated to Mariendorf DP camp where the International Rescue Committee's search for his parents proved futile.

Wearing oversized trousers belted with rope, the sleeves of his torn sweater covering frostbite blackened hands, Joseph waited at the gate in a daily vigil reminding other D.P.'s that waiting for someone you love could be as life sustaining as food.

Depressed, Sybille refused to speak, eat or rise from her bunk, seeking refuge in sleep. Unable to forget raping and pillaging Russians, Sybille could not wash away memory of the horror staining her soul. Feeling unclean, violated, her tender feelings destroyed, she felt incapable of ever again opening herself to receive a man. Refusing to live with pain, Sybille determined to die. Inga Spandau wondered how to revive her mother's desire to survive. What could she do to heal a wounded soul tormented beyond redemption? If Joseph lived with them, slept with them, shared their barrack home they would become a family offering hope for the future. Her mother would have a reason to live.

At the camp gate Inga Spandau sat down beside Joseph and placing her arm around his shoulders embraced him. Joseph pulled back, shaking his head, rejecting her. Undaunted, Inga returned the next day and told how her mother cleared rubble in the streets, how they survived air raids and starvation before being liberated. She described long columns of the homeless walking for weeks on snow covered roads, without food, shivering in the sleet and cold winter winds that killed anyone without the courage or strength to walk on mile after mile with each agonized step a journey to life…to a future. Joseph listened, imagined being embraced by his parents, memories revisited every day of his vigil. Desperate to break his silence, Inga Spandau told her favorite childhood story, Hansel and Gretel, two children entering a forbidding forest marking their return with bread crumbs soon eaten by birds. But no black forest or unmarked trail or ravenous birds appeared in Joseph's imagination as he closed his eyes seeing himself in a crowded Freight car, surrounded by strangers choking on the odor of urine and excrement and unwashed bodies. Inga Spandau described two children lost in a wilderness, searching for a way home as Joseph recalled his mother on the railroad platform, heard her calling his name as he waved and shouted: "Mommy, Mommy" --- but his cry could not be heard, his desperate words trapped in a throat forever mute. Inga Spandau described how sheltered from a storm under a tree Hansel held his sister, tenderly embracing her, shielding her from the rain. Crying out, Joseph fell into Inga Spandau's arms, sobbing. Trembling. Shaking his head. His fists striking her as he shouted again and again --- "Lost! Lost!" Pulling from her embrace, choking on tears, he sobbed - "Lost! Lost! Joseph lost!".

The next morning Joseph was gone. Inga Spandau searched the camp and learned Joseph had been transferred to a school training him to work on a Kibbutz. Devastated, she returned to her barracks convinced she would never see Joseph again. But she did hear him again. Amidst the babble of a hundred nocturnal voices Joseph's agonized cry was heard as she dozed between sleep and wakefulness. She heard only one word. "Lost! Lost! Lost!" reviving that moment when she held Joseph in her arms. One word arousing feelings she never imagined she contained. She also heard other distressed cries, other words like "God!" and "Help!" and the family names of those who would only live in dreams. Night became inhabited by unquiet ghosts never losing their power to inflict pain on the living who learn that to survive is to live in pain forever. For are we not all voices crying out in the wilderness of our lives?

As a University student, Inga Spandau joined other students eager to demonstrate solidarity with the Palestinians. Training in Libya was a more purposeful vacation than hiking the Black Forest. Learning to hi-jack airliners, make bombs, and navigate the trackless desert by compass, wristwatch and truck odometers, was an experience to talk about when returning to school.

"To kill a VIP official when he is not traveling is difficult," the Palestinian explained in accented German, scanning the classroom, aware of his student's differences. Yes. Inga Spandau thought, we are not Arabs, more like tourists playing at revolution than Jihadists willing to die for a cause. "Bodyguards always surround a stationary target forming a protective closed circle," the Instructor continued, mispronouncing German, evoking subdued laughter at his accent. "It is God's Will you understand what we are fighting for. No land! No peace! Death to the Jews!"

The Instructor turned from the blackboard and studied Inga Spandau who appeared shameless. No head scarf. Seductive eyes hidden behind sunglasses. Worn Levi's under a white cotton Galabiyya. A Harlot's voice reminding him Infidels believe Arabs are only waiters, cooks, drivers, bloody Wogs! The Instructor turned and saluted a photograph of the Father of the Nation on the wall above a sniper's rifle. He took down the gun and pressing the butt against his shoulder, aimed at an imaginary target. Peering thru the telescopic sight, he posed in front of the class as Death's Messenger. "Political power comes from the barrel of a gun," he proclaimed panning the rifle around the classroom, aiming at his audience. "One dedicated man, woman or child," he continued, "one bullet can change the world". The students were not impressed. One raised both arms in mock surrender evoking laughter. Troubled by their disrespect, the Instructor restrained his anger returning the rifle to the wall. "You can more easily kill a VIP when traveling," he continued, pausing to allow the class to understand. Turning to the blackboard, he chalk-marked points A and B connecting them by a line indicating a highway. He paused as the students studied the diagram. There were no questions. The Instructor turned and looked at Inga Spandau. A friendly glance despite knowing women are the Devil's candy. Sweet. Very sweet. But always, always, poison to a believing man's soul.

"Assume our moving target travels with a security car in front, and one protecting the convoy's rear." He sketched a three-car formation on the road. "You select a location where the motorcade stops or slows to a very low speed." The Instructor drew a circle at a right-angle turn in the road. Stepping back from the blackboard, he allowed the class time to study the diagram. "Here, at this intersection" he said, his voice rising, pointing at the circle, "here you set-up a triangular assassination plan. Here you fire from three different positions and destroy your target in a cross-fire." His hand moved swiftly across the blackboard, drawing three converging lines of deadly fire. Stabbing the chalk on the board, he shouted: "Here and only here! Allah Akbar!"

At night, before falling asleep, Inga Spandau determined to tolerate more revolutionary rhetoric, blinding sandstorms and dehydrating heat to become a Freedom Fighter. An engine of history. Yes. she told herself - here, in this forbidding desert, she would train for a cause worth dying for.

Was she dreaming? But no, still half conscious Inga Spandau awoke with the instructor in her bed, his hand caressing her breast. She lay still. Waiting for her mind to clear. Inga Spandau removed his hand, pushing him away. "Nein," she protested. "Nein." The Palestinian laughed, pulled back the blanket and lay on top of her as she tried to roll out from under him. "Nein," she cried out. "Do not do this. You must not!" The Palestinian covered her mouth with his hand as she struggled under his weight. "Infidel Bitch," he said. "Infidel Bitch." She pressed her hands against his chest. Pushing hard. "Not this way," she insisted. "Leiber Gott. Not this way." The Palestinian slapped the side of her head. "This is our way," he whispered. "You are not in Germany Fraulein." She cried out, pushing against him. Resisting. The Palestinian struck again. Her mouth filled with blood as she passed out.

Yes. This was no dream.

There were other dreams, however. Other ambitions. Without friends, estranged from family, with no permanent home, Inga Spandau dreamed of destroying decadent department stores crowded with shoppers pursuing the good life; authorities denying responsibility for Germany's moral bankruptcy; and humiliating the luxury-loving middle class living lives of quiet desperation. Fire bombings, bank robberies and kidnapping became acts of a tormented soul determined to use violence to transform the world. She became a Revolutionary. A dedicated engine of history.

Yes, she admitted, there will be many deaths. Collateral damage. But what does it matter? What is the life of one person? One death? We all live one brief moment and then die. Yes. Inga Spandau proclaimed, she will go on killing to make the world a better place to live.

On the highway from Augsburg, Inga Spandau found an ambush site. A traffic intersection thirty kilometers from Dachau where the road narrowed and turned East. A church, a garage and a vacant building provided three concealed firing positions insuring that the government Minister driving to the memorial at Dachau would never arrive. Shooting from a garage window, the first gunman would initiate the attack as Inga Spandau fired from the Church doorway. On the roof, the third marksman would cover their withdrawal. Reviewing her plan, she carefully re-assessed placement of the gunmen attacking when the convoy was most vulnerable. With the sun rising behind them, blinding the bodyguards, they had luck. A good beginning. Overhead the slow tolling of the Church Bell counter-pointed the beating of her heart. Killing Politicians who betrayed their plundered country was her mission. It was her duty to eliminate men who led Germany from catastrophe to catastrophe, Goose-stepping to drumbeats, blindly marching one step forward into disaster, two or three back to oblivion, always laughing, applauding, intoxicated by a belief in a national destiny that made the hatred flow. In twelve years Germany's soul vanished up the chimneys. In the putrid smoke rising from the Death Camps Germany discarded the intelligence, culture and humanity that civilized the Hun.

A mile from the intersection, a reflection of sunlight on a windshield signaled the approach of a black Mercedes limousine. Without a security car preceding the convoy, Inga Spandau hesitated. Her resolve weakened - thinking – one car traveling alone does not feel right. Raising the microphone to her mouth she ordered: "Hold fire! Hold Fire! Do Not Fire!" as a streak of flame propelled a grenade from the garage window striking the Mercedes without exploding. The limousine stopped, hesitated, then accelerated around the corner towards the church. Inga Spandau stepped from the doorway aiming at the tall, startled passenger behind the driver. Her automatic fire shattered the windshield killing him. A second burst wounded the driver who fell against the steering wheel as the car swerved into a tree, the horn wailing a single high-pitched note as the bodyguard in the front seat struggled to open the door. Inga Spandau stepped into the street firing through the side window killing him. A flawless attack, except for the dud grenade.

So. Let the hatred flow.

The taste of freedom was in the air as Baruch Lev walked through the Englischer Garten, Munich's inner city park. Casual strollers shared footpaths with cyclists and joggers, while on the benches beside the road, long-haired Hippies, Pensioners, and young lovers made him envy everyone enjoying life without fearing the unexpected. In Europe, discarding a Kibutznik's brusque manners was essential. Being inconspicuous in crowded cities made him feel safe although footsteps following his walks did arouse paranoid feelings. He never strolled past a store window without searching for the reflected evidence of a Tail. Someone loitering near him evoked fear. One evening, a slow-moving limousine drove past him without a passenger, the Chauffer looking out the side window as if searching for a house number, then driving off, red tail lights blinking as the car pulled to the curb and parked. Baruch Lev crossed to the opposite side of the street, his heart pounding. Danger aborted the pleasure of walking the streets of a free city as a free man. A feeling he would never enjoy again for he would never live a normal life. He would forever be following a labyrinth of clues with each new path leading him to other informants in pursuit of war criminals for whom pardon or amnesty was unthinkable. No Statute of Limitations would save men guilty of crimes against humanity for the past is never past and must be confronted if it was not to be repeated.

As evening twilight darkened, Baruch Lev turned off the footpath and rested on a roadside bench. Breathless, feeling faint, his pulse racing, he was aware of his age. He now fought his war in cafes, hotel lobbies, parks and street corners seeking informants leading him to war criminals. His generous payments for information attracted defectors, the stateless, and con men who served both sides of every conflict. He was confident he would find useful tongues for in Munich originated orgies of death and destruction, hijacking airliners, fire-bombing department stores, and kidnapping government officials. Here, Terrorists enjoyed sanctuary from a complicit government as they competed for weapons and financing, with political statements written in blood. Violence was the language they spoke.

Baruch Lev studied the strollers walking through the park memorizing faces. Some were familiar, walking or jogging at predictable hours, while others never seen before, triggered caution. An unfamiliar face walking past, head turned away seemed threatening in the deadly game of spies spying on spies. As his strength revived, Baruch Lev walked down the path to the Eisbach to watch nudist bathers escape the summer heat. Their lean bodies sun bathing on the beach inhabited a world where fear was on holiday. Baruch Lev's longing to share their lifestyle intensified as he recognized he would never live the life he was observing with such envy. He felt he would someday die alone forbidden by the heartless game he was playing from bonding with others. Everyone was capable of deception. Betrayal.

Reflected from the surface of the water a narrow blaze of sunlight silhouetted the tanned bodies of the nudists lounging on the white sand. Innocent children at play. He could not escape a world where assassinations and lies were commonplace. The nudists descended from another world of Gods and Goddesses come down to earth to show mankind what it is to be human, to worship beauty and truth, to defy death. Tears filled his eyes. He turned and walked from the beach knowing he was grieving for his own lost self. The man he once was who is no more. Someone who could think and feel and was free to act on his thoughts and feelings without restraint.

Returning to the park bench Baruch Lev regained his composure watching pedestrians walk past. A lonely task until Inga Spandau sat down beside him. Startled by the intrusion, he recognized her. "I watched you watching me at the beach," she said, smiling. Teasing. Laughing. "Did you like my tits?" she asked. Embarrassed, Baruch Lev nodded as his mind rolled back. Then fast forward. The Hitchhiker. The Café. The fashion model. What did she want? he wondered, his caution light blinking. "I'm no Peeping Tom," he said. She laughed and pointed at the crowd walking to the river. "That beach is in every Guide Book. Attracts more tourists than the Zoo."

"Good to see you again," he said, recalling the drive from Dachau, the outraged customers in the Café.

"Still selling oranges," she asked interrupting his thoughts.

"Yes. And you?" He replied. She laughed. "I'm between jobs. I don't have the new look. Designers have abolished women's bodies. Something they have no feeling for. Only flat chests are fashionable."

"How sad," he said. "A future without breasts."

"Yes. The final genocide. But tell me. Why the tears?"

"That's a long story."

"Tell me. I love long stories."

"I wouldn't know where to begin."

"Well then," she said, rising from the bench, "I must be off. I haven't run my miles today."

He watched her as she leaned over to stretch her thin long-legged body before running off, as graceful as a cat about to pounce a prey. He did not ask her to stay and sit with him, or respond to her warm greeting. There could never be an innocent encounter.

Yes, it's the Jew, Inga Spandau confirmed as she ran down the path, head back, mouth open, breathing deep. She enjoyed the feelings aroused running through the woods, her body more alive with each stride, the park's fresh air, Munich's Green Lung intoxicating as wine. She was happy to find her quarry, another easy mark she would play like a violin. No matter how hard they try horny Kibbutzniks can never appear European. Like Samson in her favorite Bible story who couldn't stop looking at breasts which probably explains why Delilah blinded him. She laughed at the thought thinking few men could resist a good fuck. A stiff prick has no brain. Men lie, parade, fight and die leaving women to birth, suckle and raise more cannon fodder. But no more. That will change. Her battlefield was a bed and her web woven of words, sighs, and sexual promises. Her unchanging scenario never failed to seduce hostages. Televised, the dead evoked horror for a few days, but live hostages held the world's attention for weeks, months and sometimes years. Yes. Freedom is worth fucking for. Her defiant statement to a corrupt world. A world refusing to look at injustice. A world accepting exploitation of the weak and enrichment of the powerful. A world of perpetual wars begun by criminal leaders devouring the young. A world preferring evasions, lies, and illusions. A world that was doomed.

She would encounter the Israeli again stopping to talk for a few minutes, arousing his interest before running off, aware he wanted her to stay. She recalled the drive from Dachau how he enjoyed their discussion. Seducing him would take perhaps months of painstaking guile. She would wait several days before returning to the Englischer Garten where she would swim and sunbathe on the Eisbach beach before jogging to the bench to find her easy mark.

Yes! I seduce randy diplomats, attract gay Englishmen, and bed unwashed Russians trading sex for information in Munich where I learned Frenchmen are lousy lovers, Americans easy victims, while Israelis tall or short, handsome or homely turn me on. Perhaps because I remember my Bible stories about the Chosen people. The children God loved best. I am also chosen to do what I do because I know what can be accomplished by violence. I also hate the intellectuals who failed to teach what it is to be human and remembering Hitler's thousand year Reich, I hate Germans with no marrow in their bones, or faith in their souls who goose-stepped to destruction applauding and cheering until the world woke up and stopped the bastards. Germany can never atone for their lies, intrigues, illusions and deadly ambitions. They made me a hopeful citizen of a new world where justice prevails. A world where the few cannot exploit the many, where tomorrow is not hostage to the past. As a Russenkinder, conceived by rape, I believe what has been divided shall one day be reunited by violence so terrible we will recoil from the horrors perpetrated. The more devastating the disorder the sooner we will choose something else. At night, when morbid images arouse my rage, lightening discharges from my brain, a firestorm of anger leaves me weak and spent, unable to stand when I rise from bed. I stagger to the stove, brewing and drinking black coffee, smoking a cigarette, sitting and contemplating my life. A book divided into chapters: Refugee. Displaced Person. University drop-out. Activist. Terrorist. Seducer. Each chapter increased my ability to defeat loneliness, because loneliness is a hammer blow that shatters glass but hardens steel giving me the power to be different. Striving to be what no one else can be, seeing the world as it is and hopefully can become. I will embrace the world like a lover and expect no easy return of my love. I will accept pain and doubt, the price of achieving my best hopes knowing what will survive my death is my love for humanity.

    I will never forget my mother, a Truemmerfrau, one of thousands of "Rubble Ladies" clearing streets and avenues of our cities, the Gotterdammerung of Germany's fantasy of glory and conquest. Stone by stone, brick by brick, these women buried Germany's heart under ten million acres of the remains of shattered buildings, unmarked tombstones recalling man's futility; while women, yearning for their love, worried and wept, waiting for their return from war. Never again, never again will women applaud and cheer our warriors. Never again will we raise our sons to hate another mother's son and allow them to march off to war to kill some other mother's darling boy.

"The arc of the moral universe is long but it bends towards Justice."

Martin Luther King

THE NEGEV DESERT

Ahamed Haddad shaded his eyes with one hand to scan the highway for the dust cloud of an approaching car confident he would succeed in collapsing the bridge. No problem when the charges were properly placed. Waiting under the hot desert sun, the sky and sand merged at the horizon creating mirages. He thought about his people holding on to their land by the Will of God and the destructive power of dynamite. Yes, indeed, the Israelis build well. But, as it is written – the desert conquers all. Moving sands cover all footprints. Ahamed Haddad inserted blasting caps into the drilled holes connecting them to a battery. Lighting a cigarette, buttoning his tunic against the cold he squatted on the sand and waited. Yes waited. Always waiting. Waiting for an end to roadblocks and killings, an end to closures, check points, curfews, humiliation, harassments. Confiscations. Settlements. The Bulldozing of homes. The uprooting of vineyards and olive groves. Waiting for an end to everything illegal. Immoral. Obscene. No more. Please God. No more! Allah Akbar! No more waiting!

As a child he herded his Grandfather's goats providing milk and cheese for the market. At noon, when the sun was most cruel, Ahamed Haddad moved them into the village seeking shade. At sunset, sitting beside his Grandfather, he watched the water bubbling in the Hookah, listening to stories of the Will of God. Insha'Allah. Yes, it was God's Will his father washed dishes in a Cairo kitchen returning home for the evening meal, prayers and a brief moment of passion in the brass bed that was his mother's dowry. Insha'Allah! It was also God's Will one morning his father did not rise from bed as the cocks crowed and the Primus stove lit as it was every day. In the street below their window, fouling the air with exhaust fumes, a Bus waited for his father sounding the horn once, twice, three times before driving off less one passenger. Yes. As always. Insha'Allah! God's Will.

"We are an ancient people," Grandfather began another story, "Older than the Koran. Older than Father Abraham. Older than all the tribes growling and spitting at the Jews. Our Sheiks, Kings and Generals are only the droppings of the British and the French. As it is written – from Camel dung you cannot make honey cakes."

Sunlight climbed to the top of the Minaret. Shadows darkened the narrow street. In shaded doorways merchants in long white Abbayas sipped coffee and sucked on water pipes watching an emaciated donkey scavenge the ground for food. Grandfather turned and pointed his water pipe. "Donkey!" he shouted, "You will only find what has been dropped by the Will of God. A kernel of grain if it is so written. For that is always Insha'Allah!" Yes. It was God's Will that one day Ahamed Haddad waited on tables in the same restaurant where his father worked. "Bloody Wogs!" was the usual response to service. Never a please or a thank you. Rude arrogant Colonials sipping pink gins explained everything in angry voices shouting "Bloody Wogs!" with smug superiority. "Bloody Wogs!" explained their loss of an Empire and failed careers to disappointed administrators living on inadequate pensions. "Give a Bloody Wog a MIG and they will crash," they said, laughing. "Bloody Wogs can't fly, shoot or run their stupid country".

Yes. Ahamed Haddad learned, humiliation is the most painful of all wounds.

"I want a life worth living," said the young Palestinian addressing a sympathetic audience, pausing to sip from a coffee-stained cup. The crowd murmured assent, greeting his words with raised fists and applause for lunch hour was the time to drink dark sweetened coffee and listen to inspiring speeches. Arab refugees fleeing their occupied homeland crowded Cairo's cafes. Few found jobs. But all, listening to impassioned rhetoric, cheered the speaker. The Palestinian continued: "In refugee camps we only exist," he said. "All we ask is to sit under the same fig tree as our Fathers and their Fathers before them. All we ask is to raise our children in a land we call our own." The audience stamped their feet. Shouted. Sipped coffee. Nibbled honey cakes. Ahamed Haddad put down his cup. Grandfather was also a man of words. Inspiring words. Sacred words. Words that speak to every generation. Sharper than swords are the right words. True words. He fought back tears. Agreeing with the speaker. Yes. Yes. I want to live a life worth living. Not merely exist. The Palestinian, his voice rising, continued. Making poetry of thought. "Until we have our own nation we will never stand among men as equals. Never. We will deserve contempt. If we fail, let it not be because we are Bloody Wogs. A man who will not fight for his birthright, truly is a Bloody Wog!"

As the car arrived at the center span of the bridge, Ahamed Haddad detonated the charge dropping car and bridge into the ravine. Airborne, the car fell into the dry river bed, rolling over as it landed, four bright steel hubcaps spinning like demented eyes in the evening's fading light. Ahamed Haddad scrambled down into the ravine, to the wheels grinding on fractured bearings, the odor of scorched rubber, gasoline and oil fouling the air. Baruch Lev, dangling from his seat belt, groaned. Ahamed Haddad lowered him to the ground and then carried him to a truck on the highway. He placed him inside, kneeling beside him to support his broken arm. The door closed. The engine labored as they drove a rutted desert track into the night. Ahamed Haddad struggled to stay awake, half-conscious until the door opened admitting fresh air. He saw a mine shaft house where a large cable-wheel mounted on a high steel tower turned slowly. He carried Baruch Lev to the open Lift, carefully supporting the broken bone bulging below the shoulder. The elevator plunged into darkness, scraping the shaft walls as they dropped to the floor of a Mine where a kerosene lamp illuminated a chamber furnished with a small wooden table, cots, a primus stove, and a stack of military ration boxes. Ahamed Haddad lifted Baruch Lev on to the table, cut open the sleeve and examined the arm. There was little blood.

"I have set many broken arms," he said. "This will not be difficult."

Eyes glazed, uncertain of what he heard, Baruch Lev nodded.

"I have nothing for the pain," Ahamed Haddad said. "I'm truly sorry." He trimmed the lamp brightening the room. Grasping the broken arm, his fingers slowly pulled apart the bones. Baruch Lev groaned. Ahamed Haddad hesitated, concentrating. Again he attempted to separate the break. "Relax," he said in Hebrew. "You must help me." His fingers slowly separated the bones. The lamp flickered. The fractured ends snapped into alignment. Ahamed Haddad nodded. Smiling. "You are a brave man," he said. "With much courage." Ahmed Haddad leaned over and gently bound the fracture with adhesive tape. To support the arm he fashioned an over-the-shoulder sling with a towel, stepped back and admired his handiwork. "There," he said in Hebrew, "This should hold you for awhile. You'll soon be as good as new."

Baruch Lev tried to sit up. Ahamed Haddad reached down and restrained him. "Take it easy," he said. "If you stand you'll fall."

Baruch Lev, his mind clearing, stared at him. Now fully conscious he complained, "You wrecked a good car."

"Yes, I know," Ahamed Haddad said, "Collateral damage."

"You must be crazy." Baruch Lev said. "You try to kill me and now set my arm?"

"Neither insane or mad. Just doing what I've been trained to do. I'm a Doctor." Ahamed Haddad turned and walked to a cot at the back wall of the chamber returning with a thick wool blanket. "Here," he said, covering Baruch Lev's shoulders. "You must stay warm. Keep you from going into shock. Keep you alive."

Baruch Lev laughed, shaking his head. "No one will give you a dollar for my life," he said. "My government doesn't reward kidnappers."

"Your prisons are overcrowded, " Ahamed Haddad said. "One Israeli can be exchanged for many of my brothers." He again reached out and carefully adjusted the blanket. "You must stay warm."

"You swore an oath to do no harm."

"True," Ahamed Haddad replied. "Your University taught me to save lives, heal the sick, bind up wounds and restore health to everyone."

"Accomplished by dynamiting bridges and murdering the innocent," Baruch Lev replied. Ahamed Haddad paused ignoring the remark, then spoke as if at prayer. "For too many years my people have suffered from a soul-destroying illness, a lingering chronic disease of the spirit called the Occupation. The Calamity. The Naqba. I hope to cure them of this disease before it becomes terminal. And I will continue until we learn not to hate each other, learn to peacefully raise our families, plow the soil, harvest what we have sowed for our endless wars corrupt our souls, corrode our spirit, defiles everyone while no heart, Arab or Jew, remains unstained. I want to make good all I have promised my children hoping that someday we will know peace, find glory as brothers, for two nations are in thy wombs, said the Lord to our mothers."

The Palestinian pointed at the G.I. cans along the wall next to an old army cot. "There's good water," he explained cordially. "Food will be sent down tomorrow," he said, pausing for a response. Baruch Lev, agonized by his painful arm, sat up on the bed and stared at the Palestinian. "Fattening the sacrificial Lamb?" he asked provocatively. Ahamed Haddad smiled. "That's a question for your government to decide," he replied, draping the blanket around Baruch Lev's shoulder. "You're not worth anything to us dead," he continued. "So stay calm," he ordered and then turned and stepped into the Lift, pulling on the control cable suddenly disappearing up the Mine shaft like a vanishing apparition. Baruch Lev, his injured arm throbbing, his mind clearing, listened to the rumble of the elevator's cables reminding him he was isolated from a world he might never see again. Held captive in an escape proof prison accessed only by a mine shaft, Baruch Lev wondered how long would he be here? Weeks? Months? Years? He knew negotiations for his release could be mired in details delaying agreements. After several deadlines, talks often end with exhaustion for the negotiators or death for the hostage. Not a comforting thought.

He knew solitary confinement would not break him; knew how to live with his thoughts taken down from the shelves of memory, ideas, books, songs and remembrances of a young Kibbutznik working under a blazing sun dreaming a dream, driven by hope. His memories would sustain him in this windowless Tomb eight paces long and six wide testing his will not just to stay alive but also coherent. He measured the dimensions of the chamber. Eight paces from the cot to the back wall. Eight back. Twenty eight feet. Ten times up and back, 280 feet. A hundred round trips 2800 feet, times two hundred trips, a mile, and every mile one more hopeful step towards survival. Like the evacuations of starving Concentration Camp prisoners fleeing on frozen feet on snow covered roads wearing only thin blankets, driven West by their SS guards to avoid liberation by the Russian Army. Their Via Doloroso a journey from Auschwitz to Buchenwald, from Bergen-Belsen to Dachau, from Majdanek to Mauthasen, from Sobibor to Treblinka, struggling to stay alive for over two hundred miles. Were they Christs going to Calvary? Or sacrificial Issacs saved by God? He had no answers. He had no words for such questions. He had no patience with Talmudic brawls. He recognized the power of words. Us?…Them?... Life?…Death?.. And time?... Without a watch how could he distinguish day from night? Weeks from months? Months from years? Wars were his life's calendar. Telling Time by wars. 1944. 1948. 1956. 1948. 1967. 1973. Wars and gravestones. A mother's tears. A mourner's Kaddish. A

Shofar's wail. He paced from the cot to the far wall, head high, back straight, a warrior on parade like British soldiers singing and marching to the beat of a dozen drums. He began to sing and march each step timed to the rhythm of the music in his head. His spirits rising, his eyes tearing, he sang in a full-throated voice a popular marching song: "It's a long way to Tipperary, it's a long way from home, it's a long way to Tipperary to the dearest place I know….Good bye Piccadilly, so long Leicester Square…it's a long long way to Tipperary….and my heart…yes… my heart is there."

The next morning, the descending Lift platform awoke Baruch Lev. The cables groaning under their load recalled human cries, indelible memories. He sat on his cot, his mind clearing. Looking around the chamber he located the commode, walked to it and relieved himself beginning his first day as a prisoner to be followed by how many more days? He could imagine headlines, hear hysterical commentary on TV – "War hero hostage!"… "No negotiations possible!" … "Nation outraged!"….Yes, the Prime Minister could forfeit his life. For what is one soldier's life sacrificed to save millions? Yes, what is one life worth? He knew the answer. Alive, the world would be more aware of the Palestinian demands. Dead – he became an acceptable loss demonstrating Arab inhumanity. So which side was he for? The enemy keeping him alive? Or a government accepting his death?

Ahamed Haddad stepped out of the Lift carrying a small video camera. He reached out offering his hand to Baruch Lev. "Did I hear you singing as I rode down the Lift? He said cordially. "Are you happy to see me?" Baruch Lev turned away refusing to shake his hand. "You have a splendid voice," Ahamed Haddad said. "I do enjoy those old marching songs. They stir the blood. Make the heart beat faster. Reminds me of the British Mandate years when I was a boy." He reached up to adjust the Lantern brightening the room. Baruch Lev returned to the cot and sat down, raising one hand to shield his eyes from the light. "Perhaps someday you will sing for my camera?" Ahamed Haddad said. "Your people will be happy to know you are alive and not suffering."

"My arm hurts," Baruch Lev said. "No gain without pain," Ahamed Haddad replied as if offering an original thought. "No gain without pain. You had a clean break set properly. Time heals all wounds, you know. And I rarely lose a patient."

"I am not reassured."

"With no infection there is nothing to fear. You've become a bargaining chip against a government refusing to negotiate. They can release our prisoners or sit Shiva for you. Damned if they do. Damned if they don't. We can play this game forever."

"Why don't you end it now?"

"We hope for the best. Hope for an end of injustice. From being occupied. Humiliated. Even ignorant slaves hope for freedom. The hungry for food. The weary for rest. Hope is the engine of life driving us into our future. Without hope despair would destroy us. Why go on living if nothing changes? Hope makes it possible to endure what cannot be cured. Hope is the answer to the eternal question of life or death."

"My people know all about hope," Baruch Lev said. "We have learned to be careful about what we hope for. We hoped to settle here and find refuge from death. We hoped for lives free of fear. Ordinary lives with ordinary problems. Food. Clothing. Shelter. Marriage. Childbirth. Justice. Injustice. We hoped to remain faithful to our heritage. To be human. To show compassion. To hate violence. To repudiate force as a solution to problems. To admire gentleness, kindness and modesty. To have faith in the ultimate victory of reason and morality. All we hoped for has been diminished by the struggle to survive. Instead of compassion we learned to hate. We fight endless wars instead of relying on reason and morality. We have brutalized our children. We have become outlaws defying the good opinion of a hostile world."

Baruch Lev anticipated The Prime Minister's defiance of demonstrators, the media attacking his refusal to negotiate while maintaining a status quo that was neither war or peace but political theater. A conflict paid for in flesh and blood and the nation's future. Baruch Lev knew his role, his moment on stage recalling the words of other hostages pleading for release. Reaching up to adjust the flickering gas lamp he counted the ration boxes and water jugs. He then turned to the wall to read messages from prisoners. Voices from the past. Their names and sad farewells to friends and family failed to raise his morale. On the wall above his cot a Star of David was inscribed - "Be silent. Die with honor."

Yes. His future would be determined by the Prime Minister. He would remain silent as the weeks became months and the months became years. He had no other choice. Hearing the Lift descending the shaft he turned from the wall and lay back on the cot. The Doctor stepped out of the Lift, placed a video camera on the table and turned to examine Lev's bandaged arm. "How do you feel?" he asked.

"I've felt better," Baruch Lev replied.

"Well," Ahamed Haddad said. "Without pain there is no gain."

"You've said that before."

"Yes, I know," Ahamed answered. "All great truths are worth repeating."

The doctor sat at the table facing Baruch Lev and turned on the camera. "Today I want you to ask your government to negotiate. In this way you can choose to live for your country rather than become another sacrifice in our endless wars."

Baruch Lev stared into the lens shaking his head. "I am a soldier, " he replied. "Not a turncoat. I will not make propaganda for you."

"Cooperate and you will be our last hostage," Ahmad Haddad said. "There will be peace when your government agrees to negotiate."

"We don't believe that."

"What is the alternative?" Ahamed Haddad asked. "Mutual assured destruction? Fighting the same battles with the same outcome for seventy years? Is that what you want?"

"We want peace with honor."

"That was said before and begat more war."

He missed seeing stars, clouds and the ever changing sky. Reminders of the world he once inhabited. Gone were the joys of sunrise or sunset, the feel of the sun on his skin, the sights and odors of market places crowded with vendors hawking their goods. He felt half alive. Without darkness to distinguish night from day his sense of time vanished. His daily calendar was the wall where other prisoners scratched marks for each day recording their despair. Sanity depended on managing time, the endless days. He could be captive for years. He divided days into hours pacing the chamber, hours thinking, singing, reciting poems and remembering; at night he dreamt of a world where men could live without ideologies. He was living a nightmare that could destroy his mind. He feared this more than death.

Ahamed Haddad untied the towel supporting Baruch Lev's arm and removed the bandage. "You heal well," he said. "You have good bones." After weeks of solitary confinement Baruch Lev welcomed a visit. Turning the camera on the Palestinian reached up and adjusted the overhead light. Removing a cigarette pack from his pocket he opened it with surgical skill offering and then lighting a cigarette for Baruch Lev. "Why not fight another kind of war? Why not fight for peace? Not tomorrow but now! Peace now."

Baruch Lev remained silent.

"Thirty two years ago your government signed a treaty saying they would recognize the legitimate rights of Palestinians and establish an autonomous authority in the West Bank and Gaza within five years," Ahamed Haddad said. "And nothing happened. Nothing changed."

"Making nothing happen is often the best choice." Baruch Lev said.

Ahamed Haddad continued. "Eighteen years ago at Oslo your government said we would conduct talks to achieve final status agreement within five years and nothing happened. Nothing changed."

"We were partners in deceit," Baruch Lev replied. "Collaborators serving different political objectives."

"For years your government said the father of our country was the remaining obstacle to peace. He died. Nothing happened. Nothing changed."

"And the whole world pretended the peace process was real," Baruch Lev said.

"Your government said if the Terror stopped there would be peace. The terror stopped. Nothing changed. Your government doesn't want peace while we will no longer will live without freedom. No longer accept lies. The truth is your government does not want a Palestinian state."

"Do you?" Baruch Lev replied. "Your leaders rejected our generous offers."

"Tell me my friend, to what and when will you ever say yes?"

Awakening in the middle of the night, not yet conscious, Baruch Lev opened his eyes and saw grotesque shadows dancing on the walls, strange images formed by flickering lantern light, moving shapes accompanied by music he never heard before orchestrating a mad choreography. Waving arms and dancing legs twisted and turned on emaciated bodies, misshapen heads and unseeing eyes nodded and laughed keeping time to blurred doomsday images evoking paralyzing terror. Overhead the revolving Cable wheel raising the Lift moaned and groaned like a tortured human voice. The foul odor of the commode and his unwashed body reminded him he was a hostage and the images on the wall unreal. Though continued isolation can induce madness he had not lost his mind. He rose from the cot and stepping to the mirror studied the dark stubble on his unshaven face thinking he must ask for a razor. Neatness and discipline maintained self-control. Small details mattered. He returned to the cot and lay down, covering himself with a blanket determined to sleep. Or, if sleep did not return, he would rest halfway between wakefulness and sleep. He would think about a past that is never past but is with him always. He now knew the answer to his father's question. They were indeed Goliaths ravaging David's impoverished land wielding a sword that cuts both ways, wounding both victor and vanquished in bloodshed that precluded peace. Every great dream has a great price and payment cannot be postponed or evaded through endless negotiations. And he also knew how much he had changed. A Kibbutznik who once labored in the hot sun, joyfully singing and dancing to greet each new harvest now thrusts his bloodied hands into another man's soil calling it God-given destiny. When asleep he would dream of other possibilities, other promises, and when awake he knew they were beyond reach of men driven by greed and fear and power. He remembered nights sleeping under the stars, the air perfumed by flowering fruit trees, hiking the Biblical trails of the Promised Land. He remembered his frail adolescent body hardening into manhood. Strength that once accomplished wonders now crippled by moral failure. He knew he could not cast off morality's imperatives. It saturated the air he breathed for someone raised on the Commandments, and when transgressing no act of confession could erase shame. He recalled the haunting faces of Arabs retrieving whatever possessions they could from the wreckage of their homes. And he also remembered not seeing hatred but the resignation of an ancient people accepting their fate as if it was a natural event willed by God. Insha' Allah explained their catastrophe. Their Naqba. His catastrophe was made by man. Wars of Choice. Yes, the Chosen People did not choose well. And this he could not deny, could not evade seeking answers to the question: who will end the curse of the Occupation and answer the Talmud's cry. "If not me - then who? If not now – then when?" He prayed for the possibility that men crying no more war can make a difference. He would now refuse food insisting there is no alternative to Peace. His death would challenge governments to negotiate. He would risk his life for peace.

Ahamed Haddad stepped out of the elevator and walked across the room setting a camera on the table in front of Baruch Lev. He reached into his long white cotton Abaya and gave a script to Lev. "Please record this message," he said, "It can save your life." Baruch Lev returned the script. Haddad continued. "You should realize who are your friends. Who is most concerned with keeping you alive."

Baruch Lev laughed. Shaking he head. "I cannot read this."

Haddad rose from the table. Reached up and adjusted the lantern. Brightening the room. Smiling he asked, "You prefer to die?".

"If necessary. I'm not merchandise you exchange for murderers."

Haddad nodded and pointed at the camera. "Freedom has a price. A debt you can pay with these words."

"Those are not mine," Baruch Lev replied. "I am a soldier. Not an actor. I cannot perform for you."

"And what do you call your fasting? A bed-time story?"

"An act defining who I am. What I fought for. How I die must be my choice."

"You do not have that option."

"My life is in my hands."

"Our lives are in God's hands," Haddad said, "Insha' Allah."

"Not my life" Lev replied. "Not God's Will but my own. There is a time in a man's life when he must bet on himself, staking his life on the outcome. There is one moment on which his entire future turns demanding all his strength. All his courage. If he fails that challenge his life becomes not much more than piss water."

"And this is your moment?"

"I will fight for peace in my own way."

"A foolish death," Haddad said.

"I believe my death will arouse our people and give Peace a chance."

"A remote possibility."

"If you allow me to speak it may happen."

"And what would you say?" Haddad asked. "What would you say that has not already been said."

"Turn on your camera."

A blinking red light was Haddad's only reply.

Baruch Lev spoke in Hebrew and Arabic. "Being of sound mind I offer my life for peace saying - the killing must end. We must make peace now. Let us not kill more of our young and generations not yet born. For sixty days I will fast, for sixty days my body will slowly consume itself. As you watch me die, you can determine my fate saving my life by saying: - No More War! No More War! Demonstrate. End the killing of our children and our children's children. Take command of your lives and our future by insisting - Peace Now! Turn from the darkness of lies and denials. Return to the Rule of Law where Justice restrains power. Have courage and we can save our people worthy of our great heritage. As my body consumes itself, my heart weakening, my mind becomes more alive as my heart empties of its fear. We talk of peace and make war. We shout: "Death to the Arabs!" "Death to the Jews!" and fill Detention cells with our brothers. Scientists say radioactive fallout decays in ninety-nine years. But what is the decay rate of our hate?

Is hate our fate?

Baruch Lev did not rage against the dying of the light. Ravished by hunger, he drifted in and out of consciousness with indifference. Clouds of memory floating through darkening skies recalled victories, defeats, regrets, hopes and aspirations of what he might have been, had he lived a different life. With his senses intensified, the lantern hanging from the ceiling became a dazzling sun, the center of his vanishing existence. The elevator shaft's squealing cables revived memories of the lingering sorrows of war; screams and cries for help ending in death. His end no doubt, for he was expendable defying glory-seeking Generals, slaying Philistines again and again and again, doomed to never learn. Mad Samsons igniting Pilars of Fire! Burning! Burning! burning in orgies of mutual destruction. Scorpions trapped in a bottle killing each other.

Despite vowing to sacrifice his life for peace, Lev was destined to live! Rescued by Doctor Haddad who descended from the elevator to raise Lev from his death bed, disguising him in a long white Abaaya cloak and checkered Kaffiyeh. "We must flee," he said. "You are in great danger." Lev lifted his head from the pillow, opened his eyes, staring at Haddad, struggling to understand. "You are to be executed by Madmen " Haddad said. "Decapitated and videotaped to make publicity." Lev shook his head. Attempted to speak. Haddad continued. "Like a sandstorm, Jihadists obliterate everyone in their path." He lifted Lev's emaciated body from the cot carrying him to the elevator to rise him up into the bright desert light offering the possibility of life. "Unlike your intransigent Prime Minister, I will not let you die," Haddad said.

In silence, seated on a donkey, riding out into a wasteland of shifting sand dunes contoured by hot winds making each breath an agony, Lev slowly regained strength, feeling at home in the desert night looking at the stars. Familiar constellations guiding his journey. Reading the skies he would never feel lost. With Orion, Scorpio, and Polaris overhead he never felt alone. Never a solitary, fugitive escaping fate. Haddad followed an old Camel track into the desert. Lev struggled to stay upright in the saddle. "We must keep moving," Haddad said. "We can only travel at night." Lev remained silent, studying the skies. "We are not the first fugitives fleeing for their lives on this route," Haddad said. "Unlike the Via Dolorosa, this way leads to life, not death." As the eastern horizon lightened and the stars overhead grew faint, desert sand gave way to small stones and gravel as they descended into a deep canyon walled by a high rock escarpment. "In ancient times," Haddad said, "survivors of devastating wars destroying their civilization hid here to keep alive cultures that might be lost to all but memory." He helped Lev dismount and led him into a large cave. Removing rations and blankets and a lantern from a saddle bag he said, "There is a spring at the back of the cave. We have food, light and water."

"Essential to civilized life," Lev said.

"You might say that. Man, I believe, doesn't live by bread alone. Man is a resilient animal. Civilizations come and go. Man does more than endure. He prevails. When the final Holocaust obliterates all evidence of our great empires, nations, states, and religions, destroyed not by atomic bombs but by mutual self-destructive hatred, there will still survive testimony, carved on the walls of caves, of an inevitable tomorrow. I'm sure you agree, tomorrow is a good idea."

With each sip of water and mouthful of bread Lev felt life return dissolving a cloud of unconsciousness. Encouraged by Haddad, Lev's appetite revived, banishing starvation. Sleep became as nourishing as food, restoring strength. And when Haddad wakened him raising him to his feet to take his first faltering steps Lev felt gratitude to a Savior no longer seen as an enemy. "When you become stronger," Haddad said, "We will continue our journey." He embraced Lev holding him erect on trembling legs. After walking the length of the cave, Lev lay down, falling into a deep sleep welcoming a brief escape from fear. Dreaming, he often felt the exultation of a warrior dominating battlefields, protecting his people from unrelenting enemies. Awakening, all illusions vanished, the taste of defeat in his throat. Awakening revealed the truth. Peace was an illusion. His death a futile sacrifice.

As stars rose in the evening sky a Camel Caravan arrived at the cave, an ancient way point on a hazardous journey crossing the Negev desert. Loud voices and the pitiful moans of camels folding their legs as they kneeled and were unloaded awakened Lev. Haddad welcomed a band of Bedouins who carried their bedrolls into the cave and unrolling a rug on the floor, lit a water pipe filling the room with fragrant smoke. Inhabiting a world without Time, Bedouins live by a tribal honor code mandating hospitality to strangers. Plates of boiled mutton and bowls of couscous were spread on the rug, a leather wine bag passing between the diners who ate and talked and smoked as if they were all brothers. Lev ate and drank and laughed with them, sharing fellowship with an ancient people who counted every mouthful of food a blessing, each day a gift. With humility the Bedouins displayed a gratitude that Lev recognized as the wisdom of the centuries. The Bedouins listened sympathetically as Haddad explained they were fleeing for their lives, for Bedouins were also outcasts smuggling to feed their tribe when the desert's barren soil failed to sustain their sheep and goats.

"Ahlan wa sahlan. Welcome," said Sheikh Hussein the Caravan leader. "Ism Allah. May the name of God protect you."

"Kattar Kheirak," Haddad said. "May God increase your bounty. Increase the good that comes from you." Sheikh Hussein, a Tribal Chief nodded, acknowledging the blessing. "You are not the first refugees crossing this desert to the sea," he said, "Nor will you be the last fleeing from the wars consuming our Land." He paused, sucking a mouthful of smoke from the Hookah. "The good given by Allah is now being destroyed by mad dogs devouring each other. Only Allah knows which dog is most vicious." He passed the water pipe to Haddad who paused a moment, comforted by the perfumed fragrance of Hashish. "We thank you for your hospitality," Haddad said. "It is our way," Sheikh Hussein replied. "We can do no less and remain who we have been since the beginning of time." He stared at a rising puff of smoke as if recalling the past. "Bedouins also dream of one nation of many people where Koran, Bible and Torah live in peace. In '48 and '67 we fought beside our Israeli brothers only to have our grazing land taken from us. Our herds no longer feed our nomadic people. And now we smuggle to survive." Haddad remained silent, nodded and turned to hand Lev the water pipe. Lev raised the pipe to his lips closed his eyes and inhaled. After a moment of pleasure he returned the pipe to Sheikh Hussein. "One day we will right that wrong," Lev said. "My people are capable of justice when properly led." Sheikh Hussain put down the pipe and speaking with subdued anger said: "Your leaders have no honor. No dignity. No respect for Bedouin traditions. Our way of life. My people are nomads, herders of sheep and goats and with no grazing rights cannot survive on land they have occupied for centuries. Your government compels my people, accustomed to life under the stars, breathing clean desert air, to live in cities where they become homeless drifters. What good is it to read and write while ignorant of the wisdom of the desert? Why is the evil your people do so commonplace it is not recognized as evil anymore? How did peace become your enemy and war your only choice?" As if responding to the voice of a Muezzin calling the faithful to prayer, Sheikh Hussein turned to a wall of the cave and kneeled. The Bedouins raised their hands to their faces, touched their foreheads to the ground and prayed. Lev turned and walked out of the cave, inhaling the cold night air to clear his mind. Looking up at the stars he recalled his troubled feelings watching Rajoub pray, reminded his life was incomplete. Bereft. Lev recalled few sacred words from a childhood that taught him a secular faith. Yet he still possessed a personal testament, his own soul's ecstasy, confident no enemy can batter down the far flung ramparts of his mind.

At dawn the Bedouins awoke, drank cups of hot tea, kneeled and said the morning prayer. Rolling up the rug and bedrolls, they reloaded the Camels who protested their burdens with tormented cries. Joining the smugglers, Haddad and Lev traversed an ocean of sand and stones crossing one sea to another that hopefully would provide a pathway to freedom.

Seated on a camel, his head wrapped in a Burnoose, Baruch Lev felt seasick climbing the crests of Dunes rising and falling like a relentless sea. Riding past mounds of animal and human remains, seeing piles of sun-bleached bones reminded Lev the unconquered desert is a cruel enemy. Never a friend. The Caravan followed a poorly marked track with foot prints of previous travelers erased by the ever-flowing sand. At dawn, stopping to eat and sleep and replenish their water bags from ancient wells, Lev enjoyed a few hours free of the torment of a hard wooden saddle. Guided by Bedouins, travelling after dark, Baruch Lev counted the days of their journey by the setting of the sun when they folded their tents, rolled up their sleeping rugs and resumed their trek in the cool of the night. Fighting the desire to sleep, Lev swayed back and forth in the saddle, his eyes heavy, almost closing. Haddad rode up awakening him with sharp jabs of a riding crop. "If you fall off and are hurt," Haddad shouted, "the Bedouins will leave your bones for the jackals and hyenas." Lev laughed and shouted a reply, raised his riding crop and exuberantly slashed down on the camel's side. Haddad continued a plodding pace knowing their lives depended on the endurance of their camels. Riding through the desert night, alone with his thoughts, mesmerized by the undulating motions of the camel, Lev felt he was lost in a waterless sea of sand with only the stars overhead connecting him to a world he may never see again. Abandoned by his government, hostage to an unknown fate, fleeing execution, his life saved by his enemy, Baruch Lev consoled himself thinking whatever will be, will be.

Later, resting in a tent they shared, Haddad served their daily water ration, set aside the canteen, and looking at Lev said: "Insha' Allah my friend. As it is written in the Koran, the future is ordained and not ours to see." Baruch Lev raised a cup of water to his lips, drinking slowly, shaking his head. "I do not understand why you accept without question Insha' Allah? Why our fate should always be in God's hands." Haddad smiled and raising his voice said. "Life will show you the truth, my friend. God is Great! Greater than your wisdom or mine. Allah Akbar." Baruch Lev smiled. Put down his cup and said: "Why then have we been given Free Will?" Haddad paused, and calmly as if talking to a child explained: "We have been given Free Will to be free to believe God's holy words. Free to pray five times a day, free to fast, free to go to Mecca, free to crusade for justice, free to make Jihad, a holy cause not of vengeance or spite or hatred, but a sacred calling,"

Baruch Lev paused, hesitating before replying. Pouring another cup of water, he slowly gathered his thoughts as if reluctant to speak. "Your sacred calling kills Infidels, stones sinners and rejects a heritage that for hundreds of years welcomed and did not resist change. A culture where creativity and the rule of law and artistic glory thrived enriching and embracing and not attacking neighbors. Today Your Jihads breed poverty, violence and exclusion from the modern world. The freedom you describe wastes the talents of women, denying believers the freedom to think, speak and determine their lives. Your faith demands obedience instead of allowing freedom to make choices. Good or bad. Truly a belief for a people ruled by fanatical Imams and not their individual conscience.

Haddad remained silent as he pulled back the Burnoose uncovering his head. He stared at Lev a moment. Then his voice changed. "The world has had enough of choices. War and not peace. Colonialism and occupations instead of granting the dignity of self-determination for what you call the turd world. You choose to live and rule according to the dictates of your perverted science that produced all the horrors we are fleeing from. Man is more than an animal ruled by chemical reactions in the brain. In all of us there is something that cannot be seen or touched, or held in one's hand that survives long after we turn to dust. Yes indeed. Our Eternity is a matter of the choices we make and some people make the wrong choices."

Haddad raised his hand, interrupting Lev as he began to reply. Motioning for silence, Haddad pointed at the walls of the tent bulging inward from the increasing force of the wind. "Simoon," he explained. "A very bad sand storm." He wrapped the Burnoose around his head, covering all but his eyes. Unrolling a prayer rug, kneeling, he bent over and touched his forehead to the ground and prayed "May Allah protect us." Lev felt helpless listening to the roaring sound of moving dunes surrounding and covering the tent. Driven across the desert by hurricane force winds, Simoons build up high moving waves of sand and gravel, blotting out the earth and sky, choking lungs and blinding eyes. As the unforgiving storm buried their tent it became a Tomb where only small pockets of air contained within canvas walls sustained life. After the Simoon had past, as if taking a vow Haddad and Lev remained silent, conserving the air they breathed, aware asphyxiation was soon probable. Confronted by death, concealing despair, they held hands, aware of a growing affection, a bond, a love refusing to distinguish between friend or foe. Only their eyes peering through openings in a Burnoose spoke to each other. When the storm abated, and the sun rose into the now clear sky, the darkness inside the tent lightened as they heard Sheikh Hussein frantically calling their names. First faintly and then growing louder as they answered with desperate cries guiding the Bedouins to uncover their Tomb. Hearing his Saviors shoveling away the sand that was not destined to be his burial shroud, Baruch Lev recalled another Resurrection. The rising of the dead at the Last Judgment and he felt born again.

"To see the world in a grain of sand,

And a heaven in a wild flower,

Hold Infinity in the palm of your hand,

And Eternity in an hour."

William Blake

At the end of a long night's journey across the forbidding Negev, Lev and Haddad welcomed the first brightening of the eastern sky. At dawn they dismounted, chilled by hours in the saddle. Unloading and watering their Camels, erecting tents, they shared the Nomads' daily tasks. Wandering a land without borders, herding sheep and goats, Bedouins lived lives beyond time bonded by affection, companionship, and a respect for Sheikhs who were also tribal historians. Sheltered in Hussein's tent, Lev and Haddad were enthralled as he recited enchanting tales of his people. Raising the water pipe to his mouth, exhaling a fragrant cloud of Hashish, Sheikh Hussein paused and said with great dignity: "In the name of Allah, the compassionate and merciful, Islam is the answer to all aspects of our lives for Islam is noble and humane. All other Faiths are uncivilized, self-destructive, while Islam survives with compassion and beauty. All other religions fail, for Islam is the true faith of the desert unforgiving to those who do not live up to its laws."

Lev turned to Haddad who remained silent. Lev picked up the water pipe, closed his eyes, and inhaled. He then passed the pipe to Haddad who nodded, encouraging him to speak, Choosing his words with care Lev said: "With respect, ya Effendi, Islamist advocates death as a way of life promoting slaughter and suicide, murdering thousands of non-believers. They encourage their children to become tomorrow's Holy Martyrs teaching the only good Jew is a dead Jew."

Camels hobbled outside the tent groaned their mournful lamentations as if they overheard Lev. With only a cold desert wind blowing through the tent Sheikh Hussein respectfully nodded and speaking quietly smiled and asked: "So you are one of the Chosen people. A Hebrew?"

"Yes, ya Efendi."

"Abraham's children are always welcome in my tent," Sheikh Hussein said graciously. Then raising his hands to his face, meditating before continuing, said: "The Prophet, Peace be upon him, had respect for all people, because all men are created in the image of God. The Fanatical Jihadists you speak of are not the true Islam but a corruption taught in crowded cities where every blasphemy is permitted. They are heartless worshiping in Mosques that do not convey the Islamic spirit of peace harmony and love. Their Imams pray five times a day asking God to protect human bombs. They dress young boys in suicide vests convinced death isn't death but a beginning. For such Fanatics Paradise is life's only goal. Their religion is not the true Islam where we bear witness there is no God but Allah and Muhammad is His messenger."

They again passed the water pipe in the communion of desert travelers. Sweet tasting smoke perfumed the tent. Only the watering and feeding of Camels abused the silence of the night. "In the name of Allah," Lev said, "Jihadists choose hatred, not love. War not peace. Chaos not civilization, destroying our children's future betraying both Muhammad and Torah."

Hussein raised one hand to interrupt Lev. Raising the water pipe to his mouth he inhaled and nodded before saying: "Your people are also guilty with curfews, checkpoints, bulldozers, home destructions, land seizures, shootings, assassinations, and the building of walls. By occupying our land you've become Outcasts isolated from the goodwill of mankind."

Lev turned to Haddad who urged him to reply. Raising his voice, almost pleading, Lev said. "We are fighting for our right to exist on a land where we can live in peace with our neighbors. Certainly this is not too much to ask."

Sheikh Hussein put down the water pipe. Raising his voice he said: "Neighbors? People you humiliate and kill forgetting we are brothers. Our divided homeland cannot stand divided. We must unite as one nation under God living with respect for his Holy Word ending the bloodshed destroying our people. And my friend, Habibi, for this reason I would like you to become a Muslim. For Islam is truly the word of God, a religion for all created in his image."

"With respect Ya Efendi could you become a Jew? Could you accept the demands of our history? Our idea of freedom that defines my people. Free to think, speak and worship God in our own way." The cook entered the tent with a bowl of Couscous, set it down on the rug, bowed and blessed the food. Haddad and Lev waited respectfully for Sheikh Hussein to begin eating. He closed his eyes, covered his face with his hands, and after a short prayer reached into the bowl and raised food to his mouth. Haddad waited a moment before speaking. "With respect, Ya Efendi, both Muslim and Jew no longer believe in the possibility of change and nothing will change until we reconcile what we say is impossible. We are trapped in failure, prisoners of what we have been saying to each other for sixty years. Unless we change the language we speak, killing will continue."

"Disbelief is the enemy," Sheikh Hussein said. "Disbelief that conquers hope. And hope only comes from a belief in God's Will. Insha' Allah. So let us pray together for as it is written, Allah works in mysterious ways."

Bowing his head, Lev turned to Sheikh Hussein and said: Ya Efendi, our people are hostage to a terror destroying all that makes life worthwhile. We seem doomed to live in fear making our nightmares come true. Surely there is another way."

Lev struggled to stay awake as the Camel's undulating motions lulled him to sleep. Peering through a narrow opening in his Burnoose, studying the Stars, he felt awe and wonder watching the unchanging Universe revolve overhead. Orion's journey across the sky, Scorpio rising over the distant horizon confirmed the caravan was crossing the Negev desert towards the sea. Towards Freedom. Riding past ancient watering holes marking their route, they rode to the crest of dunes overlooking an ocean of sand inhabited by nomadic tribes who grazed their herds, birthed children and buried their dead since the beginning of time when no other voice could be heard but the mysterious tongue of the wilderness vanquishing doubt and speaking of faith. At sunrise they set up tents, watered their Camels, and sheltered from the heat, rested until darkness enabled them to resume their flight. A journey towards Truth pausing only to eat and drink hot cups of Tea and talk for hours conversing in three languages, Hebrew, Arabic and Death. A dialogue of interchangeable horrors. Demonstrations. Massacres. Suicidal Slaughters. Funerals with enraged mourners demanding revenge.

Lev spoke of Death as a way of life, of living without hope, fearful, distrusting a world in which Israelis struggled to survive as they picked up shattered body parts in the streets, despairing about their children's future.

Haddad told of humiliations, insults, indignities, disrespect, arrogance and a denial of the sanctity of a human life driving people to the edge of insanity. Removing his Burnoose he uncovered a face etched by wind and scorching sun. A Prophet's face. He stirred the glowing embers under the cook pot brewing another cup of tea. "No man should be compelled to flee his heritage," he said quietly. "The soil holding my father's bones affirms my identity. My dignity. Take my land away and I am dispossessed without honor or pride, an angry Jihadist killing to express my rage. Occupied land is no homeland but a crime, a prison with high walls where relocation is no escape but a sentence of death, where souls atrophy in despair. Denied our future we have no choice but to fight for our lives as we try to survive a terminal illness."

Haddad scooped up a handful of sand smothering the glowing embers under the cook pot, extinguishing the flames. "Your greatest crime has been giving us someone to blame for our failures. With no incentive to change we remain trapped in our feudal past unable to live and prosper in a world different from what we inherited. Your nation has been built on the wreckage of our people where young Arabs and Jews destroy their future throwing stones, shooting rubber bullets, bombing and gassing each other in mutual self destruction. An insanity that time will not cure."

Lev poured another cup of Tea and said: "Are we fleeing a sinking ship?"

Haddad said: "Remaining silent, accepting war as inevitable makes us accomplices to an evil that will only endure if we surrender to horror. What we dream can happen. My life is a dream. I have not lived as my father did, a dumb brute dying in despair serving a thousand Masters, enduring their arrogance, surviving humiliations, losing hope. I found solace in the Mosque where I learned to read and write and pray for a better life. Insha' Allah! It was God's Will an illiterate became a Doctor and so I say what you wish for is no dream but can be a reality."

Following an unmarked track the Caravan traversed a sea of sand on an endless journey through a moonlit desert. Driven by prevailing winds, dunes formed rising hills and depressed valleys with only the stars providing a sense of direction. The constellations overhead were a menagerie of images; the Bear, Scorpion, Flying Horse, Centaur, and the

Bull confirming they were not wandering through an indifferent Universe but were on course to their destination. High in the saddle, struggling to stay seated and warm, Lev's companions were the whispering sands and the snorting groaning Camels plodding along indifferent to time or place. Watching the Moon slowly rise above a distant horizon Lev felt like a voyager crossing an infinite sea, his destination far from the horror he was fleeing. In an unspoken bargain with God he knew he could never escape the great mystery, could never understand his dreams or capture the meaning of a glowing star.

The sand cushioned his fall from the saddle, embraced him in soft maternal arms as he lay unconscious, face down on the side of the camel track. He had no sense of how long he slept. Awakening stiff from the cold of a long desert night he rose to his feet searching for the caravan. The horizon, lightened by the rays of the early morning sun offered no hope of rescue. He was alone without water under a blazing sky. Wrapping the Burnoose around his head, shielding himself from the daytime heat, Lev followed fading camel tracks fearing they would soon disappear under the drifting sand. He staggered forward, his boots sinking ankle deep with each step, his strength slowly ebbing from dehydration. Refusing to accept his fate, struggling to stay alive, Lev counted steps as if reckoning the distance to salvation. At a thousand steps, his mind wandering from the task, he began recounting, recalling an ancient Chinese Proverb "a journey of a thousand miles begins with a single step". Each step a life sustaining achievement. A victory over death. At sunset, after resting in the heat of the day, the Bedouins would resume their night time journey making it impossible to follow and rejoin them without water to sustain life. Then a Miracle! Lev saw on the horizon ahead, shimmering in the heat haze, a large lake bordered by flowering Palm and Acacia trees. He saw wind-driven ripples flowing across the water and in the center of the lake a bright red ball of fire mirroring the mid day sun. Yes. A Gift of the Gods! He rushed forward, almost running, pursuing his receding vision with cries of joy. He staggered. He fell. And rising to his feet tore off his clothes and plunged into the cooling waters of a mirage.

When he awoke, his naked body wore a blanket of sand. He opened his eyes, looked up and saw Haddad holding him in his arms, brushing the sand away, putting on his Burnoose, shielding him from the blistering sun. Raising the water bottle to his parched lips Haddad said: "Slowly, slowly, you must not drink too much, too fast." Lev sucked at the bottle greedily. Haddad pulled the canteen away. "You will vomit and die if you drink too fast." Lev fell back and closed his eyes. Nearby a hobbled Camel, smelling water, snorted and shuffled its feet. Haddad erected two short tent poles, covering them with a ground cloth, shading Lev from the sun. "Tonight, when you regain your strength, we will find the caravan." Reassured of survival, Lev fell asleep dreaming of his childhood comforted in his mother's arms. Now lovingly embraced and saved by his enemy he saw the ways of God are beyond understanding.

At dawn, after brewing the morning coffee, raising the cup to his lips Lev said: "Shukran! Thank you very much!"

"Afwan, il Afu," Haddad said, "You're welcome."

Outside their tent Bedouins murmured morning prayers. Footsore camels kneeled and moaned as the sun slowly rose heating the cool night air. "Tomorrow, God Willing, we will cross the Border and find Freedom," Haddad said. "And then?" Lev asked. "We will live new lives," Haddad replied. Lev put down the cup and unrolled his bedding. Folding his legs under him he sat down on the floor of the tent. "Will you continue fighting for your people?" Lev asked. Haddad nodded and said: "I have no other choice. Jihad defines me. Being a Jihadist is how I fulfill my destiny. Within me are both the dark forces of Evil and Allah's sacred words and I am the battlefield where they fight. My agony is intense. I love my soul and do not want it to perish. Only through Jihad can I become a whole man for I am both good and evil, spirit and flesh." With the rays of rising sun shining through the tent wall behind him, Haddad's face was concealed in darkness. His deep voice rose passionately saying: "When Life as an occupied people becomes unendurable, Intifada is our only path to freedom."

"We need more time, Lev said.."

Haddad nodded and said: "You want more time for winning while losing your reputation for morality. More time for continuing your incredible prosperity while perishing as a democracy. Certainly fifty years of such self destruction is enough time."

THE PRIME MINISTER

A "Most Wanted Criminal Poster" on the wall, behind his desk reminded visitors during the Mandate years the Prime Minister led the Irgun Terrorists. Rejecting the nonviolence and diplomacy of recognized Zionist leadership negotiating with the British for statehood, the outlawed Irgun Freedom Fighters bombed buildings, bridges and railroads believing in the Biblical injunction an "Eye For an Eye". Retaliating for the flogging and execution of Irgun Fighters they flogged and hanged British soldiers. Denounced as a fanatic, defying world opinion, jeopardizing the birth of a nation striving for recognition, the Prime Minister never abandoned his God-given mission. After years of relentless Irgun insurgency and assassinations, the British surrendered their Mandate to govern Palestine enabling a return to a land without people, a people without land. After years opposing more moderate governments, the Prime Minister transformed Israel, dividing an already divided nation. He encouraged settlements in the occupied territories while initiating Wars of Choice to insure national survival. Never questioning his judgment, dismissing all dissenting opinions, he asked his cabinet: "What is the price for the life of one Jew? One soldier? What is today's price? Or tomorrow's? Or next year's? No one answered. He shook his head and continued. "Exchanging Baruch Lev for Palestinian prisoners would make us accomplices to their crime. Our soldiers are not merchandise to be traded when convenient." He looked around the room, staring at his audience, his eyes revealing a soul on fire. A short, frail passionate politician, the Prime Minister turned to his Advisors and struck the desk with his fist. "We will find and free Baruch Lev. Negotiating admits weakness when we must show strength." Waiting for a response from the men seated around the table he hesitated. There was no dissent. He walked to the window and looked down at the demonstrators. Removing his glasses, rubbing his eyes, he said: "There can never be a war without suffering. We must harden our hearts. Do our duty." He raised one hand as if attempting to silence dissent. Shaking his head he said "Bleeding hearts, Bleeding hearts". He turned to his Advisors and insisted "Meeting their demands admits defeat. Without sacrifices there can be no history." Raising his hand again he said: "Thousands of prisoners have been taken from us and we survived." He again pointed at the street demonstrators. "We must stand up to this test of our will not only by our enemies but also by citizens willing to jeopardize the future of our nation to save someone they love. If we respond to their demands we will have many more hostages. We will be extorted again and again. Gentlemen, we have no choice but to say without hesitation, no deal. Never."

Chief of Staff General Posner, reluctant to disagree said: "We will lose a brave soldier. Are we not obliged to rescue our boys no matter how high the price? Can we allow them to rot in prison for months, perhaps a year?"

"It will take as long as it will take," replied the Prime Minister. "They will not kill Baruch Lev. He is of no use to them dead. We will not empty our prisons of murderers to free one soldier. To make one family happy." The Prime Minister raised a hand as if blessing a congregation. "We have lost many good men," he said. "No one can defeat soldiers who refuse to accept defeat. Men who chose victory or death! Sacrifice, courage and the death of twenty thousand such men made this nation. They never surrendered their principals no matter what the world demanded. They never compromised. Never waited for anyone to give them their birthright. They fought for their rights and were victorious. Lev's entire life was part of that history and he will do his duty. I have no doubt he will agree with our decisions. He is a Sabra."

The Prime Minister shaved soap and stubble off his cheeks before examining his pale thin face in the mirror. After brushing his teeth and combing his hair he put on a clean white shirt, a dark necktie and a black suit for he never wore open-necked shirts and a workman's cap. His old-world European appearance shielded him from the British during the Mandate Years. After a breakfast of Tea, toast, an egg and a sliced orange, he entered an armored limousine greeting the driver and bodyguard as familiar friends. Driving to his office he read the daily newspapers troubled by the news. The Zionist dream had faded. Car and real estate advertisements and stock quotations displaced stories praising hard work and sacrifice. Greed had corrupted the Israeli soul.

"Hold fast to dreams, for when dreams die, life is a broken-winged bird that cannot fly." For members of Betar, the Zionist Youth Organization he once led, this poem sustained dreams of a nation extending from the Euphrates to the Mediterranean, including both banks of the river Jordan. Drafted into the Polish army during WWII, shipped to the Middle East, he deserted and settled in Israel to build that dream. Working to lead his people back to their heritage, his nights were tormented by a history of failures; decisions and actions that could go wrong went wrong. In recurring dreams he often climbed Mount Sinai to find the strength and courage and the will to do what he thought right no matter the opposition. In his mind he climbed the mountain where it all began convinced his nation will someday follow him. His great task was unfinished. He had not yet earned the right to die. That so many die at his command was heartbreaking. He would forever be haunted by the unquiet ghosts of Sabra and Chatila never banishing from his memory the machine-gunned dead covered by flies; women, young men and boys, babies, grandparents, shot in the head. He would never forget hospital patients butchered in their beds. Mounds of flesh and blood, legs and arms entangled. His most famous General deceived his government and their American Allies, disgracing his leadership. He could not forgive himself for trusting someone so unworthy of trust. Soon he will resign, go home, lock the doors, pull down the window shades and sitting in the dark, think long and hard about his failure, praying for redemption.

Nights were for thinking, not sleeping. Disturbing images kept him awake until dawn when he left his bed to begin his day. Turning on the light he looked at his hands trying to control the trembling. Fear had become an unwelcome visitor. Cold sweats dampened his bed clothes and when he went from under the covers he felt not fully alive. Turning to the open window to watch the day begin, he said the morning prayer thanking God for the gift of this day and for making him who he was. With five armies poised to destroy his people he then prayed for the miracle predicted by True Believers who called him – "King of the Jews". His enemies called him paranoid. Bowing his head, he recited the ancient prayer; - "May my right hand wither if I forget thee, Oh Jerusalem." He would never cease fighting for his people. As a young man he crossed a treacherous sea to build a nation from the ashes of Europe overcoming all compromisers, peaceniks, intellectuals, journalists, and do-gooders to save his people from resignation and despair. Yes. One day he will earn the title – "King of the Jews".

Secluded in his home, sitting alone in a darkened room he asked: "What kind of Jew am I? What kind of Jew have I been? Did I show compassion? Hate violence? Admire gentleness and kindness and modesty? Was I concerned for the suffering of others? Did I believe in the ultimate victory of reason and morality? Did I recognize that force is ultimately doomed to failure? Or like Old Testament Kings and Warriors did I send armies to burn down cities? Slaughter the innocent? Occupy conquered lands? I never listened to voices advocating a peace that cannot endure. I had the courage to do what I thought right regardless of being hated, scorned and detested. And I suffered doing my best for my country."

I fled from SS Death Squads to begin a new life and unlike Lot's wife never looked back at my village. Never heard my neighbor's agonized cries or watched flames consume our Synagogue reddening the sky like a burnt offering to an Evil God. I walked two hundred miles on bleeding feet through dark forests and across frozen Steppes moving East towards the rising sun away from the war slaughtering my people. I endured hunger and cold, and the fear of invading armies. At night I burrowed like an animal under sheltering trees covering myself with leaves and fallen branches, gnawing bitter roots and sucking nutrients out of whatever I could find in the underbrush. I listened to the night sounds of the forest, heard Owls calling my name, watched stars slowly revolving overhead. I awoke to the hopeful songs of birds greeting the day. Awed by the mysteries around me I accepted my fate. I was in God's hands. As my shivering body weakened from hunger hope revived. I knew I would survive to fulfill my destiny, to do my Life's work.

I have not become Prime Minister to preside over the dissolution of my country. A people hounded, isolated, and forsaken; refugees abandoned by an indifferent world, survivors hoping to rebuild their lives. I have a terrible responsibility. One misjudgment, one wrong decision can destroy our dream. So I am prudent. Calculating. With few friends, and many enemies, we returned to the land of our forefathers. We prevailed. Fighting for our freedom we learned there are things more precious than life, more horrible than death. We learned to hate. We also learned nations die from Treaties and false promises. Only God-given land can be trusted. Only land is eternal becoming the heritage of future generations who will remember our lives were bitter struggle, our deaths heroism, our sacrifices sacred, the memory of our dead eternal. We were willing to die for our own nation knowing there is no war without suffering, no revolt without casualties, no victory without sacrifices. We never surrendered. Never abandoned our weapons for a false peace. We became warriors fighting for lives worth living. Not to merely exist – but to live! L' Chaim!

Yes. I am pitiless. Devious. Unbending. How else should I be when my nation's future is at risk? My spirit was forged in ovens; hardened by the mournful cries of millions. How else should I be when one third of my people vanished? How else should I be when our existence is denied? When Holocausts recur every century? Yet I am an ordinary human being who has been blessed with the devotion of a good wife. Received the unquestioning love of a child. A mortal man who lives every day and night with pain. I read the casualty lists and cry for my people seeing the faces of all who died that we may live. I cannot forgive this loss of youth and mourn what has been done to truth. Yet see how proudly I stand. A rock. A tree. A soul that is free. A fate that rests in my hand.

Everything I am, everything I feel, everything I will ever be will not allow me to negotiate with terrorists. Fanatics attempting to hold an entire nation hostage to their demands. To them I say: No! Never! Never again!

Chief of Staff General Chaim Posner was not a Sabra. Born in Germany in 1924, he arrived in Palestine with his parents in 1936 at the start of 'a hopeful Exodus of 141 illegal ships carrying 100,000 immigrants to the land promised by the Balfour Declaration. In 1939 he served in the British Army defending Egypt and the Suez Canal. From 1945 to 1948 he participated in Israel's struggle to survive and define itself as a nation state. Trained by the British, he demonstrated the tactical and strategic skill insuring victory in the War of Independence and the 1956, 1967 and 1973 wars confirming Israel's existence. Battlefield cruelties convinced him non-violence could be more powerful than military force. Making peace better than war. Ultimately, as promised by the Talmud, truth and love will triumph over lies and hate. At Staff meetings he disagreed with the Prime Minister insisting no matter how high the price, Freeing hostages was a moral obligation.

A short, immaculately dressed old soldier in a well-pressed uniform displaying few of his many decorations for valor, General Posner spoke in a voice accustomed to respect. "You must stop demanding perpetual sacrifice as every citizen's responsibility. We came here to live, not die for a land where death is more common than struggling to build a new Zion. Today there are few families not mourning a father a brother or a son. Your policies doom our people to continually sit Shiva for their dead."

The Prime Minister raised a hand as if patiently admonishing a troubled subordinate. "I hear you General Posner," he replied. "However you forget everyone must die and to die for Eternal Israel will be to live forever!" He paused, rose from his chair and walked to the window. Staring down at the street, restraining his feelings, he lowered his voice as if describing a vision. "The stones we walk on are inscribed with the names of our dead. The air we breathe is filled with the hopes and dreams of our blessed casualties. May they rest in Peace! Survival will always demand sacrifice by each generation! When you're fighting for survival, anything goes. Even what's forbidden. In a world surrounded by wolves to live without claws and fangs and fists is to deny reality."

General Posner remained silent. He gathered his papers on the table and placed them in a leather briefcase. Walking to the door he turned and challenged the Prime Minister before leaving the room. "The whole world is watching," he said quietly. "Watching us allow Lev to die! We must negotiate with our enemy. Our respect for human life is being tested on a different battlefield. The whole world asks – where is our humanity?"

The Prime Minister crossed the room to the doorway, smiling, offering his hand. "Old friends should never part in anger. We have been through much together. And we will never exchange murderers with blood on their hands for a soldier who is a casualty of a war. If Lev dies for his dream of a Peace that will never happen there is nothing we can do to save his life. It is in his hands. Not yours or mine or a thousand bleeding hearts praying for his deliverance. You and I have sworn to defend our people against all enemies foreign and domestic and I tell you with his futile protest Lev has become an enemy of the people he had sworn to protect!"

"Protect?" General Posner shouted angrily. "Our people are dying from your protection!" Pointing at a wall map of Israel, struggling to control his voice he said: "Our nation is more than one hundred West Bank illegal settlements with red tile roofs glittering in the sun defying human decency and justice." He reached out and placed his hand on the map. "Israel is an idea. A dream come true! And protecting that dream is what we should fight for. Not for the Messianic God-given fantasies of fanatics. Not for the fears and hatreds we teach our children. And not for your absurd map of a Greater Israel. We must return to the rule of law and show respect for the good opinion of the world instead of inciting the hatred of suicide bombers revenging massacres! We who have shown mankind how to live under one God are more than a nation of triumphant warriors! Defying International Laws we cease being law-givers. Custodians of Divine Truth. Condoning torture, land confiscations. uprooting our neighbor's olive groves we betray who we are. Our promise and possibilities. The enemies we must protect our people from are domestic not foreign!"

Guaranteed to survive a nuclear holocaust, Israel's underground Command and Control Center is a high-tech marvel of telephones, computers, TV monitors, and animated wall maps displaying information from satellites and drones hovering over all neighboring states. Six large clocks show the time in the world's capitols as if hours were an enemy to be monitored and controlled. The humming sound of air conditioners in the darkened room created a feeling of expectation and disciplined foreboding. Intelligence analysts seated on a small raised platform in the center of the room, with an unobstructed view of all screens and data boards, studied the incoming flow of data like devoted Acolytes of a mysterious cult. The Prime Minister calmly listened to the daily briefing reigning over his electronic realm with passionate intensity; asking questions, demanding answers, nodding his head, graciously thanking his advisors for safeguarding their nation. With no imminent threats to worry about, the Prime Minister returned to his office and politely said good morning to his secretary who handed him a cup of coffee saying General Posner was waiting in the Cabinet Conference room.

The General rose from his chair as the Prime Minister entered. "Please sit down, be comfortable and accept my apologies for being late," the Prime Minister said, cordially offering his hand. "Today's Briefing was unusually long." Accustomed to the Prime Minister's old fashioned manners, acknowledging his gracious greeting, the General smiled and asked: 'What are you worrying about today?"

"Nothing thank God," replied the Prime Minister. "I believe we will survive for a few more centuries."

"Insha' Allah!" replied the General. "Insha' Allah! But why are we meeting again? I briefed you last week."

"Your grim assessment keeps me awake at night."

"Well it should, Mr. Prime Minister. Well it should. A truce is only a prelude to more fighting. A bloody fool's game we've played for years and now it seems we've run out the clock."

The Prime Minister turned and walked to his desk. Picking up a folder he pulled out a dispatch and handed it to the General. "Last week's casualties. Not conducive to sleep."

The General looked at the list. "Yes, Mr. Prime Minister, I agree. The numbers will be a continuing nightmare as long as we occupy the territories."

The Prime Minister returned the paper to the folder and with a pocket handkerchief began cleaning his glasses. Troubled, hesitant he said "You are forgetting your Torah lessons, General Posner. Are we not instructed to dispossess the inhabitants of our land and then dwell upon it fulfilling a Divine promise to Abraham and his seed?"

The General raised his hand pointing to the heavens. "Divine Law should not prevail over International Law," he replied quietly. "Such simplistic religious thinking teaches our soldiers everything is permitted."

The Prime Minister walked from his desk and turned to the General and said: "We are commanded to inhabit this land even at the price of more wars."

The General pointed at the Prime Minister. "Such beliefs make our battlefield victories irrelevant. How can there be such a thing as victory when we keep killing our sons and turn Israel into a state that devours its young?"

"We are fighting for our right to exist next to neighbors pledged to destroy us."

"We've become victims of illusions deadening our national conscience. Our soldiers bravery brings only more destruction. More horror. More deaths. We are not exempt from judgment by the nations of the world losing their respect."

The Prime Minister raised both hands. "Stop," he protested. "Enough already. Enough!"

The General continued. His voice rising. "We cannot make the lives of Palestinians a living hell without being sucked into that inferno. We have sanctified our state and an army that can do no wrong, and with self-righteousness and arrogance and demonization of our enemy have made negotiating and finding peace impossible."

"Enough all ready! I've heard enough!" the Prime Minister shouted.

The General continued. His anger subsiding. "We must fight for the soul of our religion and for the our moral reputation."

" I cannot accept what you are saying."

"I know. And you also do not realize teaching our children they are the Chosen has led to hooliganism and vandalism. The morality of a wild desert tribe."

Jews don't do that, I told the Commission of Inquiry. It never happened, I insisted. When God works at creative destruction the most grisly crimes are part of his plan. Stalled in a ditch on the road to Deir Yassin our armored car's megaphone never came close enough to the village to be heard. Our warnings dissipated in the hot desert wind and failed to prevent the massacre we deny. Truth must be protected by a bodyguard of lies, said Winston Churchill and he was right. We serve a higher truth writing a history where every secret is not told, every crime not punished, every virtue not rewarded, every wrong not redressed. Praying for strength that I might protect my people I was rendered powerless. I asked for health and I was given infirmity. Despite my devotion my prayers were unanswered. I served God completing the creation of our nation in six miraculous days. And on the seventh I prayed: They that wait upon the Lord shall renew their strength. They shall mount up with wings of Eagles; they shall run and not be weary, they shall walk and not faint. Yes. Torah was written by the hand of God who does not roll dice with the universe. His Eternal Law of Compensation prevails; there is a gain for every loss and though the span of human life is nothing, the man who lives that life achieves glory struggling to give life meaning. I was not permitted to choose the frame of my destiny. But what I put into it was mine. What does it matter if one day lesser men than I carry off my corpse to an unmarked Tomb with words of damnation? How I died and what I died for alone reveals who I am. As in the game of chess how I played and what I played for reveals the man. I have been called ruthless. Ambitious. Intransigent. Extremist. Traitor. Murderer. A Devil's Eulogy by those who hate me. I never ran with the cold and timid souls who know neither victory or defeat. I am battle weary. My face covered by dirt and sweat and blood knowing the triumph of high achievement and glorious failure that only comes when daring greatly. I have suffered. Been hated. Detested and scorned. But never without the courage to do what I thought right. Always doing what is best for my country.

L' Chaim! I chose Life! Only that and always, no matter the risk. I did not let my life wear away by the mere passage of Time."

"Crusading for Justice

is an act of love and honor,

not of vengeance or spite

or hatred.

Justice is a high calling,

not a low pursuit."

Charles M. Blow

MUNICH

Walking through Munich's Schwabing district past private homes and 19th century apartment buildings Pierce Barnes found little evidence of war's havoc. An ancient Cathedral's blackened ruins of hollow burned-out rubble formed a haunting memorial in shattered stone inhabited by ghosts. A Tombstone without names reminded residents of seventy tragic nights of horror. With no heroes to remember with statues or parades, one standing wall commemorated Munich's sacrifice to the Gods of war. Narrow streets lined with towering Oak trees and window flower boxes created a village-like atmosphere of small shops and cafes.

With windows opened to admit cool summer air, pedestrians heard classical music, jazz and traditional lieder confirming Munich's reputation as a City with a heart. Strolling from the Vier Jahretzeitn Hotel down Leopold and Ungerer Strasse to the Englischer Garten Barnes joined tourists watching nude sun bathers on the Eisbach beach. Their lean bodies evoked prurient adolescent memories as they bent over like carefree schoolgirls to dry their long flowing hair in the sun. A welcome respite from Terrorists torching department stores, kidnapping and assassinating Bankers and Judges. Fanatics transforming indignation into protest, protest into resistance, and resistance into murder. "It is a terrible thing to kill," proclaimed Inga Spandau. "We will kill not only others, we will kill ourselves if necessary for this world can only be changed by force." Enraged students rioted and built street barricades, throwing rocks at the police, torching overturned cars. Sending their fanatical leader to a better world would be no small achievement, Barnes thought.

"Join the Army… see the world." An invitation Barnes could not resist serving in more foreign countries than he could recall. The Army became his only family and

Munich another assignment in a career remembered for warm English beer, sour French wine, and seeing Rome and the Parthenon at sunset. Gone but not forgotten was his carefree Kansas childhood where right and wrong were well-defined, duty to God and Country clear, and the King James Bible answered all questions. He now followed new Rules of Engagement permitting extremism in defense of freedom in a war where the Duty! Honor! Country! was often violated and Honor hard to find.

The deserts around Fort Hood, Texas, are traversed by Arroyos, dry riverbeds seasonally carrying flash floods and torrents of mud later churned to dust by military vehicles. During simulated combat exercises, Arroyos concealed tank formations before they emerged to swing around opposing units in triumphant encirclements. After a day of search and destroy tactics, Lt. Robert Miller was confident. Umpires assessing his leadership would score him high. Driving his jeep along a sand and gravel riverbed, he shifted gears, slowly climbing the side of an Arroyo where he cut the engine and set the brake. Above him, silhouetted against the night sky, a row of Sherman tanks awaited dawn, engines idling, exhaust fumes fouling the cold desert air. Chilled in the night wind, Miller buttoned his parka, pulled the hood over his head and leaned back in his seat. His Battalion, parked on the ridge above him survived the night by perfuming the air with the pungent odor of Pot. Distant thunder's low rumble awoke him as he imagined a line of rain squalls driving tall anvil-shaped clouds across the barren Texas plains, flash-flooding Arroyos, churning sand into impassable muddy-brown maelstroms. Then, aware the sound was not thunder or rain, Miller opened his eyes looked up at a cloudless night sky to see a massive steel hulk rolling down the slope towards him, clanking metal treads crushing gravel as the Tank's cannon pointed up at the stars at the instant of his death.

    Seated at his desk in the Infirmary, Pierce Barnes read the Coroner's report, walked to the sink and puked. Miller was a damn good officer, he recalled. Their undercover mission secure. How did this happen? They were not careless. Never seen together. Tongues only talked to them at Sick Call. So who the hell outed Miller? He walked to the pharmaceutical cabinet, signed the inventory and zeroed the lock. Yes. Miller was not the first wasted undercover Agent. Nor the last. Entering the door's keypad code he switched-off the lights. Everyone, no matter how cautious, gets burned. A bad joke to die Stateside after surviving Korea. Barnes secured the infirmary door and walked to his car in the parking lot where three soldiers standing under a flickering streetlight waited for him. Sergeant Small, six foot five, two hundred fifty corpulent pounds capable of angrily puffing out his cheeks when terrorizing recruits, stepped out from under the light blocking his path, an open switchblade in one hand. "Too bad about Miller," Small said, as the soldiers moved in. "Ain't healthy knowing you, is it Barnes?" Another switchblade flashed open. The three soldiers laughed. Small stepped closer. Barnes pulled a gun from his pocket and aimed at Small who raised both arms in mock surrender. The soldiers slapped High Fives. Hooting and hollering. Enjoying the confrontation. "Well, well," Small said. "Looks like I gotta put you on report, soldier," he said, shaking his head. "Possession of an unauthorized weapon. A class A offense." Pierce Barnes returned the gun to his pocket. Small puffed out his cheeks. "Ain't in no hurry, are we fellas?" The soldiers nodded. Another round of High Fives. Small grinned. "Like Renfroo of the Mounties I always gets my man. And that's the mother-fuckin' truth." The soldiers returned to their car. Small followed, sliding behind the steering wheel, racing the engine, two open exhausts roaring contempt. Small cranked down the window before driving off. "Walkin' round Fort Hood can be hazardous to your health, Barnes. This here's my turf you're fuckin' with, and what's more, no Brass goin' lay his ass on the line for you! No way!" The car raced off, burning rubber as Pierce Barnes struggled to control his shaking hand.

Yes. Yes. He shouted at the car. This is one hell of an Army. One Hell of a God damn Army!

"Possession of an unauthorized weapon," Captain Cuneo decreed. "A Class A offense, soldier. I'm going to rid Fort Hood of guns, knives, fruits, freaks and pushers." Barnes remained silent. He would postpone calling Control until he knew what this piss-ass Adjutant knew. The little bastard was definitely not informed. "Another dead G.I. is one too many," Captain Cuneo continued, lowering his voice, smiling. "I need your help. Barnes. What do you say to a little protective custody? Time to think? Maybe you'll help us get other Pot Heads." Barnes remained silent, thinking the son of a bitch could I.D. him with a phone call. What's his game?

The Admissions Nurse was adamant. No Records. No admission. Small protested. Pointed at Barnes, tottering spaced-out, held up by the MP. The nurse handed Small a phone. "Get his records, Sergeant. That's an order." Barnes reached out and grasped the Nurse's hand. "I'm sick," he mumbled. Fighting nausea. "I'm going to puke." The Nurse raised her arm. Pointed. "Down the hall," she said. "First door on your left." In the bathroom, his mind clearing, Barnes went to a telephone. Dialed. Listened to the ringing. A recorded voice, a beep. "Barnes at Darnell Hospital reporting a class 'A' emergency," he said, his voice breaking. Leaning over the sink, Barnes puked, rinsing his mouth with water as Small entered. "Got your records, soldier," Small said prodding him with a baton. Herding Barnes to the door.

At the Admissions desk Small argued with the nurse. "He's a voluntary admission," he said. "Sign your name soldier," the Admission Nurse ordered. Barnes leaned over the desk struggling to steady the pen. "Your fuckin' name, Barnes," Small said. "Just your name." The nurse placed her finger on a line on the register as Barnes scratched an illegible signature. "Please," the nurse said, examining the page. "Try to do better." Barnes steadied his hand, carefully signing. The nurse nodded, waved them away as Small escorted Barnes to an elevator door held open by a tall MP. The door closed. In the elevator, the MP smiled and flashing a row of tobacco-stained teeth, opened his shirt and rolled up a sleeve revealing a syringe taped inside his forearm. Small held Barnes against the wall. "That's where we'll all be a hundred years from now," the MP said as he bubbled several drops from the needle. "Pushing up the daisies. Pushing up the daisies." Barnes closed his eyes. "Now soldier," Small said in a mournful voice. "Time to say goodbye." He pressed the STOP button. The MP raised his arm, arcing the hypodermic needle down in one continuous movement as the elevator door opened, a white-jacketed Medical Orderly entered, and with a quick arm-swinging karate chop dropped the MP to the floor, the hypodermic rolling out into the hallway as another Orderly entered the elevator forcing Small to the wall, arms raised high, legs spread-eagled. The Orderly picked up the syringe, examined the unconscious MP patting the swelling at the base of his skull and grinned. "O.K.?" he asked.

Barnes nodded. "Next time," the Orderly advised, "Call sooner."

Pierce Barnes awoke at the Brooke Army Medical Center overlooking a meandering river carrying grain barges downstream to the Gulf. Cottonwood trees bordered both embankments with lower branches arching over the water. He enjoyed strolling the riverside footpath past other patients lounging on the grass, relaxing in the warm Texas sun. Survivors of our country's wars sat on wooden benches staring out over the flowing stream with unseeing eyes. Some smoked, napped, read, or played cards, while others rose from their seats to urinate in the river; a few wandered the embankment picking flowers that grew only in their shattered minds. A regiment of casualties enduring life's final battle, a Triage of body and soul.

Walking Wounded, like the prisoners he liberated from Korea's Chanjin POW camp. A haunting memory of a wretched compound of log Huts burrowed into frozen soil. Abandoned by Guards to die from cold and hunger, few survived this abattoir of frozen corpses. Inside unheated Huts, the living and the dead embraced each other under excrement-stained blankets. Rows of naked cadavers, stripped of clothing to warm the living, lay frozen in death's rigor mortis, skeletons protruding from under frost-blackened skin. Lifeless mouths frozen in Rictus grins asked – What took you so long soldier? What took you so God damn long? "Holy Mother of God! Holy Mother of God!" Pierce Barnes shouted, scanning frozen faces with a flashlight, searching for a sign of life, hearing not a groan or a whimper. Only his agonized sobs shattered the mortuary silence of the Hut. He fled out of the hut into the cold. Outside, waiting in the snow, his men stared at him, immobilized by horror. "Light the Coleman stove," he ordered. "Get anyone alive out." Barnes waded through waist deep snow to the next Hut, choking on the odor of rotting flesh, searching faces with a flashlight, afraid to miss a flickering eyelid, a groan, a trembling hand. He found ten prisoners alive before staggering out of the hut and collapsing on the urine-stained snow, shattered. Sobbing.

Doctor Slavin's ingratiating voice delivered his diagnosis with what he thought ribald humor. "They found everything but boot polish in your blood," he said, underlining the Lab's test numbers with a red pencil. Barnes glanced at the results, shook his head and grinned. "How come I'm alive?" he asked. Doctor Slavin nodded and smiled paternally. "Body weight saved your ass, soldier. Body weight. You can absorb a lot and not O.D. What you need is a dry-out. Comprende?"

Barnes did not protest.

Slavin's voice sharpened. "You had more than LSD soldier. Your blood numbers are off the charts.

Barnes remained silent.

"Drugs are not the door to Paradise, Barnes. You'll return to duty when you are clean."

The Isolation Barrack's walls were papered with florescent psychedelic posters glowing under blue overhead lights. The MP guarding the door leaned back in a chair reading a comic book. High-decibel Rock and Roll bounced off the walls, drumbeats reverberating inside Pierce Barnes' head. He tried to sleep on a narrow canvas cot. The MP put down the book and asked, "How about a Pepsi, soldier?" Barnes nodded. The MP handed him a can with bubbles emerging from the tab hole. Barnes sat up, looked at the can then tilted his head back in a long satisfying swallow. Laying down on the cot, feeling cold, he began shivering, wiping his hand across his forehead as hot sweats flushed through his body. Rising from the cot he staggered across the room to a wall locker. Taped inside the door were grotesque faces. Barnes pulled down the photographs, angrily tearing them into small pieces.

    Time in De-Tox became the slow movement of slanted shadows on the wall. Shadows rising in the far corners of the room, spreading over door and ceiling, dark fingers painted strange shapes on the wall. Time was rubber-wheeled carts silently rolling down hospital corridors, aluminum food trays clattering on tables, voices shocking him awake with "How are you today, Barnes?" Time was sleep, darkness and dreams, endless journeys from one bizarre world to another he dared not, could not, name. Time became unknown and unendurable as abrasive voices returned with questions and blinding lights and when the lights were switched off Barnes saw frightening shadows tracking the passage of his days obliterated. Awakening he saw blurred faces, heard muffled sounds, indistinct voices echoing in dark passageways that brightened at the first movement of his arms and legs inside canvas restraints. Awakening, he felt himself return from illness to an innocent childlike hunger to understand what had been done to him.

    "Welcome home, Barnes," Doctor Slavin said, his voice asserting authority. Barnes struggled against restraining canvas straps. "What have you done to me?" he shouted. Slavin stepped back as if recoiling from a blow. Intimacy vanished. Slavin examined the buckles. Reassured, he stepped closer, "Relax soldier," he said, his jowls trembling. "Don't spoil your recovery." Barnes stared at the whiskey blossoms on Slavin's corpulent cheeks. "Shit, what have you done to me?" he said, struggling to move his arms inside the canvas restraints. "Why this God damn Straitjacket?" Slavin laughed. Smiling. "O.K. soldier." He turned and nodded at an Orderly who unfastened the buckles. Barnes stretched his flaccid muscles. Trembling. Angry.

"Better?" Slavin asked, placing a large manila folder on the bed. "Read your Records, Barnes. You'll see you haven't been harmed."

"How long have I been here?"

"Four weeks."

"No shit?"

"Look at your numbers, Barnes. You've been one of our toughest customers. Impressive resilience. You resisted longer that anyone. A real hold-out. Quite an achievement." Barnes looked at the folder. Read his name on the cover. A license to do God know what? he wondered. "Sodium Amytal? LSD?" he asked. "Right." Slavin nodded. "Tested only on volunteers."

"I never volunteered."

"We considered your attitude, your Record. Without involuntary subjects, our data would be skewed. Someone who knows what's happening can't be tested."

"I'm an involuntary volunteer?"

"Right."

Barnes looked at Slavin's handwritten notes describing diet, sleep deprivation and medication followed by withdrawal convulsions and an intense craving for resumed toxicity. Stapled inside the folder were interrogation transcripts stamped TOP SECRET.

"Feels like you killed me." Barnes said.

"The Russian's call it 'The little death'. Take someone down just far enough to get a response. Breakdown defenses. Abort self-discipline. Loyalties. We test only strong well-defined personalities. Well-integrated. Choose the right man and there's never a problem bringing a disintegrated Psyche back together again. Believe me, we can re-integrate a man stronger than he ever was before."

"And when you fail?"

"Fail?"

"To put the Psyche back together."

"We never fail. Not once. Believe me. Man is a resilient animal. A few days sleep, lots of food and you're as good as new."

"Out!" Barnes shouted as Dr. Slavin walked in the door. "I want out. No more head-games." Slavin read the chart hanging on the foot of the bed. Signed his name, turned a page. "How do you feel?" Slavin asked.

"Ninety years old. Jump out of my skin every time a door slams. Sit in the dark and get headaches when the lights are turned on. Have Flashbacks. See what I can't forget. Hear voices shouting, screaming. And then I discover the voices are mine."

"What do they say?" Slavin asked, opening a notebook, removing a large black fountain pen from his breast pocket. "What do your voices say?"

"Who?"

"The voices."

"What I told you. Get out! Resign! No more horror! No more! Enough!"

Slavin closed the notebook. Screwed the cap on the pen. Thoughtful. "I think I understand," Slavin said. "Another malingerer! Never would have expected it from a career soldier like you, Barnes."

"My fuckin' Psyche never came together. No way! I feel like shit. Reintegration didn't work. Not on me it didn't. It's like I don't know where I am. Sometimes I can't remember my name."

"You'll lose your pension."

"Fuck my pension and fuck the Army."

"A few more years and you're on Easy Street."

"No more. No more involuntary volunteer," Barnes shouted attempting to rise from the bed.

"Barnes, you were selected for Special Forces because you are something special. Resilient. You have experienced traumas few survive without harm. The Army needs you."

"You drove me out of my mind. Broke me. Like the Russians say. I'm not sure of who I am anymore. I feel lost!"

"Think what you've gained," Slavin said. "Strength you never knew you possessed. Inner resources to survive no matter what's happens to you. You're ten feet tall soldier and now you're scared of what's coming next."

"God damn right! What's coming next?"

"Nothing you can't handle. Soldier. Give you my word. You've experienced the worst. Total disintegration.

Disorientation of personality. Complete disorganization and regression induced by isolation, sleep deprivation, hunger and terror. You should be proud. We're proud of you. Why, Barnes, you're indestructible. Nothing can hurt you more than what you've survived. And now you want to waste what you can do for your country."

"God dam Right."

Slavin's genial light turned off. He glared at Barnes. "I guess I'm premature. Too optimistic. Perhaps you're not ready. He opened the notebook and scrawled an order. "Barnes, the army can't afford to lose you."

"Prick."

"Yes Barnes." Slavin's geniality returned. "If you're unhappy request a transfer to another station where I will personally see you get nothing but shit duty."

The Briefing Officer sounded like a travel brochure. "Friendly Frauleins, luxurious quarters, generous per diems, and for Special Forces unvouchered operational funds. Every G.I. rates Munich number one." Barnes listened without protest. He had his orders. Also "Special Duty" bonuses, the officer continued. "Commendations on your Service Record. You're not just getting your ticket punched to nowhere, soldier, you're getting the whole enchilada, a challenging Overseas Mission where the Army always takes care of its own. Right?"

Barnes said nothing. He heard that song before.

The Officer concluded with advice on avoiding bribery, venereal disease and drugs. He handed Barnes a

TOP SECRET folder explaining "Here is our most current Intel." Barnes read the cover page: Three dead, five injured by two car bombs parked outside US Army headquarters, Heidelberg. One dead, thirteen injured by three Pipe Bombs at officer's mess, Frankfurt am Main. One GI murdered for an admission pass to US Army base. Two killed in bomb attack. General Haig attacked by roadside bomb while driving to his Headquarters.

Television confirmed the Briefing. Caved in Mess Hall ceilings. Shattered windows. Naked bodies blackened by explosions. Flesh hanging in trees like strange fruit. Human remains collected in garbage bags. Soldiers searching the rubble for a G.I. trapped under a Coca Cola machine with one foot protruding. An American Colonel bleeding to death with a splinter of glass in his throat followed by a defiant Terrorist statement of responsibility:

"The people of the Federal Republic want nothing to do with the crimes of American Imperialism," Inga Spandau proclaimed. "We have learned peaceful demonstrations are useless against imperialist criminals."

And responding to such barbaric statements we began our long decent down the slippery slope of dishonor that ended in savagery. Using torture, our Army lost its soul. Shamed its uniform. Betrayed what good men died for.

The Technical Advisor was a bloodless technician in civilian clothes demonstrating diabolical skills. A parade-ground voice and buzz-cut hair revealed his military past. "Extreme Interrogation is a most effective way of obtaining information" the Advisor told a class of Special Forces as he glanced around the classroom, pacing back and forth in front of a Blackboard. "Extreme Interrogation, taking the gloves off is recommended when fighting the war on terror."

The Technical Advisor opened a black leather Attache Case, on the podium to accompany his lecture. "This convenient carry-on baggage sends high voltage shocks into the guilty, the innocent, and the ideologically unacceptable. A most effective counter-insurgent weapon." He opened the case displaying batteries, resistance coils, and a dial controlling the voltage surging through two wires to be attached to an uncooperative prisoner. "The penis, vagina, nipples, and anus are useful contact points," the Advisor continued, displaying small metal clips at the ends of two short wires. He paused to study the students reaction. Some were impressed, others indifferent. At the rear of the classroom one groaned in mock agony. The Advisor ignored him. "There are other choices – a wire to an ear lobe and another to the tongue can tell you what you want to know."

A Trainee rose to his feet, screamed a tortured cry, raising both arms in mock surrender shouting – "Enough! Enough! Tell me what you want me to say!" The class laughed, applauded, stamped their feet crying – "Enough! Enough!" ending the lecture. The Technical Advisor closed the Attache Case and stalked out of the classroom. A humorless son of a bitch.

Barnes remained seated as the room cleared. This was nothing to laugh about. If this was the future. What next? What next? A filthy job kicking down doors, arresting suspects in the middle of the night. Using terror to fight terrorists. And yes, no doubt, perpetrating this horror will have a price. How high a price he learned from his first interrogation.

Barnes paused in the doorway of a prison cell adjusting his eyes to the dim light. Seated at a small table, Colonel Ysidro, mentor to a generation of terrorists, greeted him with a dignified nod.

"Colonel Ysdiro?" Barnes said.

The prisoner raised a hand, put down his pen and set aside a manuscript. Tall, with a dark beard, he prided himself on a Castro-like appearance. "I've been expecting you," he said, in a refined Castilian accent.

"Only a few questions sir," Barnes said. "Your dossier is not complete."

"Neither is my life. I am an unfinished work."

"Your books are still in print," Barnes said, acknowledging his reputation. A revolutionary intellectual engaged with history. Author of - "Violence is the language we speak".

"Who are you. Where do you come from?" Colonel Ysidro asked.

"Kansas. My father was a farmer."

The Colonel smiled a smile often seen on wall posters. "I expected a bourgeois son-of-a-bitch."

Barnes sat across the table and removed a fountain pen from his shirt pocket, unscrewed the cap, and entered date and time in a black leather notebook. The Colonel leaned back in his chair and smiled. "Another appeal to my love of the exploited I presume?"

"Yes, sir," Barnes said laughing. A joke was always a good beginning. The Colonel's smile fading, he struck the table with his fist. "I am not your sir any more than I am your Comrade?"

"Si!, Colonel Ysidro. Si!"

"I've revised my opinion of the Proletariat's revolutionary potential. I no longer believe it ever existed." The Colonel waved away a cloud of cigarette smoke with his hand as he continued, "Only fools believe they can be revolutionaries. I am only an old fool who inspired idiots.."

"I don't agree," Barnes said.

"Violence is eternal, it will never end," the Colonel said as he stubbed out a cigarette and immediately lit another.

"Then why continue to write, to lecture?"

"A writer must eat."

"And students reading your words fight and die," Barnes said.

Colonel Ysidro nodded, a flicker of emotion crossing his suddenly aged face. "I told them to find another mentor."

"They didn't listen."

"Return to your nightclubs, I said. Play-acting at revolution has consequences. Concern yourselves with fucking, not fighting. Grow up. Become human before violence becomes a habit." Ysidro stubbed out another cigarette and withdrew one from a pack. Lighting it, controlling his anger, he leaned forward. "It is harder to live for a few than die for mankind. Dying for a sacred cause brings nothing but horror." He paused to wave away the cigarette smoke. "Yes, write Colonel Ysidro worked with violence as a carpenter works with wood becoming an engine of history killing to make a better world. Living a fucking lie!" Waving his hand, he swept the coffee cup off the table. Barnes looked up from his notepad and calmly asked, "Another cup?"

"No, gracias." Ysidro said. Pausing. After a long silence, he said: "I tried to teach what I learned in Spain's Civil War. Rage always destroys what men fight for. You become what you are fighting."

Barnes filled a page. Turned another. Writing. The prisoner wanted to talk. To be heard. Remembered.

"Students ignored me. They heard what they wanted to hear. They forgot Peasants have only one cause. Land! But students! Every revolutionary idea becomes a cause worth killing for. Spain's angry young men drenched with blood the soil that gave them life and when their fury was spent discovered they had destroyed what they had been fighting to save." Colonel Ysidro remained silent a moment before confessing, "I cannot retrieve my words."

"Redemption is always possible,"

"A fantasy for Priests." Yisdro said rising to pace the cell. Then he turned and sat at the table. "Women and children blown up in a marketplace are Collateral Damage. Paving stones on the road to power. But who redeems the perpetrators, forgives the suffering they inflict? What of the causes they killed for? Remembered by old men who recall nothing but the moment they brought death to others. To squeeze a trigger is easy. Any fool can light a fuse, ambush a motor car. But to make a life? To begin when young, to continue day by day, creating something decent, a job, a family, a home. That's all there is. And that should be enough for young men to live for. Yes! I failed to teach that to fanatics."

After a tedious day studying INTERPOL dossiers and checking current INTEL, Barnes returned to his apartment to shower and shave and dress for an evening at Hofbrauhauses where exuberant Tyrolians sang raucous songs while pounding Beer Steins on wooden table tops. After dining on Weiner Schnitzel and wine he strolled along Munich's wide avenues encountering nothing but unwelcoming faces. Only whores spoke to him. Or high-priced Bar girls. And when fanatical demonstrators burned tires and our flag smashing store windows in the Marienplatz shouting "Fuck American War Mongers" he began to question saving Germany by killing their fanatical Terrorist Leaders. Observing Inga Spandau through her apartment window from a flat across the street, she seemed a lonely Hausfrau obsessed with cooking and cleaning as if expecting important visitors. She slept late. Drank her morning coffee breakfasting leisurely on toast and jam, and afternoon read books, magazines, and newspapers. In the evening, standing at the window, arms opened wide, she reached out as if to embrace someone who was not there, staring down at the street, head bowed, waiting. Waiting. Waiting. Who and what was she waiting for? Her Destiny? Watching her for several weeks opened a door into her life and entering that door he began feeling as intimate as a lover long before they ever met. He was fascinated by how she moved about her apartment, brushed her hair before going to bed, and waited at the window with open arms as if to embrace her unseen Stalker, her Nemesis? With regret he discovered he could kill her, someone he would never hurt if it was his choice. So would he do what he was ordered to do when she no longer provided leads exposing her network? A perplexing question. He thanked God his mother never lived to see him now. For what pride would this sainted woman have in her son? An assassin. A murderer. His Holy Scripture a Target List. Wanted! Wanted! Dead or alive! Whatever happened to "Thou Shalt Not Kill" ?

"Kill Ratios", "Body Counts", tormented nightmares and threatening footsteps following him when he strolled the city were as inescapable as surging crowds chanting "Death to Americans and their Lackeys". He was a lonely shadow spying on shadows in a world where right and wrong, justice and injustice were inconvenient concepts. Also ignored was the question of who first initiated the violence and who merely retaliated? Did we always respond in proportionate ways? Flying uncooperative prisoners out over the ocean, faces concealed in hoods, hands bound behind their backs, he avoided acknowledging their humanity before throwing the "garbage" overboard. And when the "Disappeared" sank beneath the sea they took with them his own decency. He wondered what are we doing to ourselves? Will he ever be able to feel clean again?

Street surveillance was routine. Wearing a T shirt, shorts and a bright red sweatband, Inga Spandau ran down the path from the Eisbach beach every afternoon at three. Jogging past him, unaware she was observed, she stopped to again speak to an Old Priest on a bench beside the footpath. The Priest welcomed her, raising a hand as if blessing a Parishioner. Leaning over to tighten a shoe lace she spoke to him briefly before running off. The Priest then rose from the bench and followed her out of the park. When they failed to meet again one afternoon, Barnes searched for them at the beach. Disappointed, returning to his apartment he filled half a glass with Scotch, sat on the bed, and consoled by the comforting warmth of alcohol tried to understand what he witnessed.

Father Hans Hussy, winner of the Iron Cross First Class lost a leg at Verdun, his health at Dachau, and his co-conspirators hanging from meat hooks in Plotzensee prison. A survivor of the anti-Nazi "Kreisau Circle", a clandestine group of military and religious dissenters, Hussy hoped to restore German democracy after returning from war to witness starvation, chaos, and a revolution led by fanatics wearing crooked crosses. For twelve years they ruled a corrupted Deutchland where Parents, Teachers and Pastors no longer were sole purveyors of truth in a country where morality vanished in burned-out synagogues. Without civic virtue and moral courage, resurrecting old Germany seemed an impossible dream. Failing to remember their history he believed Germans cannot learn from experience sliding down the slippery slope of hatred into Violence. He became a "Worker-Priest" sheltering drug addicts, prostitutes, and the homeless in a church basement, serving potato soup and black bread to Displaced Persons without identity papers, providing sanctuary for the human flotsam of population transfers. Regardless of ideology, they were God's children. No one beyond salvation, beyond redemption, beyond the possibility of change. And then one day he lost his most precious possession, the indefinable power he acquired prostrating himself on the sanctified floor of a Cathedral. Turning to his Parishioners he was struck mute. The sacramental words of the Eucharist no longer rose from within his soul. He could not raise his arms to elevate the Host, or look into eyes bright with faith, or listen to voices raised in song and prayer. Unable to continue his Priestly office he defied his superiors serving God in his own way. The way of the renegade.

Ego Te Absolvo! Can I give God's forgivness with these sacred words? When Inga says forgive me Father for I have sinned should I give her absolution? Ego te absolvo! Can killing be forgiven by saying - go and sin no more to someone who repeats her sin and asks for absolution? What a farce. Kill. Confess. Receive absolution and kill again. Am I her accomplice? Because I say the Gospels are the answer to violence, to the failure of a Christianity that fails to serve the poor, I am called "The Red Priest." Yes. What sort of Priest am I? Have I lied with every prayer? Has my vow of obedience aborted the conscience of someone who saw wrong and tried to right it. Saw suffering and tried to heal it. Saw violence and tried to stop it. Yes. What sort of Priest am I? I love my Parishioners who lost their faith only after being bombed into rubble. Divided and occupied, they suffered a guilt no prayer, no contrition can erase. So why confess? Why absolve?

Yes! Why confess? Inga Spandau asked herself. How can I be absolved when I fail to tell my Confessor everything? No act of contrition can erase memory of the ecstasy I feel dispensing Justice. The Florist looked at me with questioning eyes when asked for a dozen White Roses. "White Roses?" he replied, trying to recall where he had seen my face before. "Not this time of year," he explained. "Today you can have all the Reds you want, after all, a Rose is a Rose you know." I walked to the door, turned to him and insisted: "I'm looking for White Roses. Only White." He raised a hand asking me to wait. Then as if reading my mind he nodded and smiled a sympathetic smile. "I understand. White Roses to remember them. Yes? It's good you young people never forget". I paused in the doorway. "The flowers are for an old man's birthday greeting. Someone's Grandfather." As I stepped through the door he called after me. "Tomorrow. Come back tomorrow. I will find you Whites for your memorial. It's good you remember the Scholls. They were also Freedom Fighters."

In 1943, brother and sister Hans and Sophie Scholl led a dozen Munich University students in the legendary White Rose Movement distributing anti-Nazi leaflets and painting their proclamations on city walls saying: "The German name is shamed forever if German youth do not rise to take revenge! Down with Hitler! Long Live Freedom!" Deeply religious, rejecting violence, armed only with words, the Scholls opposed a lawless government until they and four co-conspirators were arrested, tried and executed. 21 year old Sophie Scholl's final statement to her Judge when sentenced to decapitation inspired student resistance in other German cities. Defying the demand for silence she said with great dignity: "You know as well as I the war is lost. Why are you so cowardly you won't admit it?"

Today, brave words without action are futile. Now is the time for violent protest! For demonstrations. Street theater. Fire bombs and assassinations. Now is the time to make history with our rage. Allow our hate to become our prayer. Our call for action! Today we say let no crime against humanity go unpunished as we remember the Presiding Judge's verdict forever engraved on the unforgiving German conscience!

Years later, on his birthday, we gathered at the Judge's apartment door singing our congratulations and best wishes while Gretl his granddaughter presented him a dozen white Roses. A softly strumming guitar accompanied our song. The delighted old man raised both hands, standing in the doorway, a smile brightening his gray parchment skin. His eyes seemed young. Still possessed of the fervor that pronounced sentence on countless victims of Nazi terror. As Gretl handed him the flowers, a bright red spot appeared in the middle of his forehead, just above the eyes, a small gunshot wound slowly growing larger as a crimson curtain of blood streamed down his face as he fell back into the apartment holding a dozen white roses in his lifeless hands.

Yes. The past is never past. It is with us always. Painful memories. Pierce Barnes remembered when Death swept the countryside like a Tsunami. With foliage chemically obliterated by Agent Orange, he had an unobstructed view circling over a Vietnamese village in a Helicopter, assessing the day's Body Count. The roar of engines in his ears drowned out all thought but estimating the number of doll-like bodies strewn across the rice paddies below. Hovering over a burned-out Hamlet, he identified men, women and children as enemy VC, their lifeless bodies becoming unquiet ghosts inhabiting the desolate landscape. Shouting into a microphone he reported the number of dead, his words fading in and out.

"Say again!...Say again! ...Say again!" demanded the Base Controller. "Repeat!...Repeat!...Repeat!" crowded the air waves with the futile narrative of war. It seemed they would never run out of villages to devastate, or casualties to count, or body bags to send home; and with no light at the end of this tunnel Barnes felt no grief. Only the sudden visceral shock of killing; horror followed by recognition that something inside him also died. Flying back to the Base Camp he recalled an old song, the rhythmic throb of whirling Helicopter rotors accompanied the lyrics he sang in a wistful voice: "I didn't raise my boy to be a soldier, I brought him up to be my pride and joy, who dares put a gun on his shoulder, to shoot some other mother's darling boy?"

Yes. Shameful memories of Body Counts and Kill Ratios last forever. To acquire information Executive Renditions transported Subjects of high Interest from a country where the Rule of Law prevails to another where torture delivers what we need to know. Pierce Barnes questioned this new way of making war asking; -what am I when obeying these orders? Am I a criminal killing or kidnapping on demand? Facing a Court of Justice would I plead Guilty as charged, or not guilty due to extenuating circumstances? War is a bloody horror, Your Honor. Mass insanity more prevalent, more natural to mankind than those intervals between wars called Peace. So how should I plead?" Certainly there will never be a War Crimes Trial for Generals determining accountability and responsibility. With no one guilty of anything but following orders ours but to do or die, ours not to reason why.

Barnes never felt at home in Munich. The unfamiliar language. The different manners. The foreign cars. The window-shopping tourists crowding the sidewalks in search of bargains made following Inga Spandau difficult. Keeping her in sight, matching her long athletic strides and brisk pace sometimes seemed she was aware of being followed and was testing him. Walking from the Englischer Garten to the Swabing district she turned and entered a narrow street of small stores and without hesitation entered a Bakery. Barnes walked past the store and glancing through the doorway saw her standing in a short queue at the counter. Barnes entered a shop at the end of the street and looking out the window waited until Inga appeared carrying a string bag containing a large loaf of bread and a bottle of wine. Did she see me, he wondered? He followed her past the old Prinz-Carl-Palais. A reminder of former glory, maintaining his distance as she entered the Hofgarten and walked to a large block of black granite, a dignified memorial in the center of the garden. She stopped to read the inscription on the stone bowing her head as if at prayer. Opening the bottle she poured wine into a small cup, and performing a familiar ritual, raised the cup to her lips. After drinking the wine, she placed the bottle at the base of the monument and remained motionless for a long moment of silent reflection, Barnes did not follow when she left the garden. He walked to the stone, leaned over and read the inscription.

IN MEMORY OF

"Hans und Sophie Scholl"

Fighting for freedom the Scholls rejected violence believing words more powerful than guns.

Every human life as a whole shows the qualities of a tragedy, and we see that life in general consists only of hopes gone astray, thwarted plans and errors recognized too late.

                        Arthur Schopenhaur

A narrow alley separated Father Hussy's church from the school where cheering students ran and dodged and circled each other kicking a battered football across the schoolyard. Their triumphant cries were an odd background to the long line of alcoholics and drug addicts waiting in the alley for a bowl of potato soup and black bread. Overhead, a tolling bell rang out noontime as the basement door opened admitting an impatient crowd to food, warmth and sanctuary. Without identity papers, not registered for civic welfare, drop-outs from life's endless misery survived for one more day. In a car parked across the street from the church Pierce Barnes waited for Inga Spandau to appear and enter the alley carrying a small back-pack. Wearing a blue anorak and hiking boots, her face hidden inside a hood, she seemed like another Wandervogel student descending on Munich in summer. Barnes stepped out of the car, locked the door and crossed the street. Unshaved for several days, a dark gray stubble covered his cheeks and chin. He wore a torn sweatshirt. Dark trousers and workman's cap. An old man seeking a meal. Entering the church he picked up a soup bowl and spoon from a table at the basement door and joined the silent supplicants waiting to be fed. At the far end of the room two large cooking urns gave off tantalizing odors of hot soup. As the line moved closer to the serving table, he could see Inga Spandau fill bowls and hand out bread with sympathetic words and a smile comforting the homeless. She seemed at peace with the world as she reached across the table to serve bread and soup to the famished. Watching her feed the homeless he observed new feelings energizing her work. After weeks of discreet surveillance he had seen from a distance only a terrorist's enraged face. Repellant as an Interpol photograph. Viewed up close, her beauty surprised him. Ruthless or innocent, she became more than a name on a target list. As he raised a spoon of hot soup to his lips, and thoughtfully chewed some bread, he realized sending Inga Spandau to a better world would be painful.

I turned my head away reluctant to look at the homeless old indigent in front of me. I gave him bread and filled his bowl without revealing I recognized him. His workman's cap, tattered sweatshirt and shuffling walk could not disguise the tall, robust American whose attention I was aware of. Yes. I confess, after weeks of constant surveillance he became someone who interested me. Another admirer to attract, seduce and torment. A lover's game played to make my day more interesting. I easily evaded his surveillance for I knew which Cafes had rear entrances enabling me to escape and leave him waiting outside across the street. I played both the clever cat and devious mouse leading my pursuer into the U-Bahn subway onto a train, returning to the platform as the door closed and he went off without me. A small victory in my war with hypocrisy.

Portrayed by the media as perpetrator of car bombing, hi-jackings, kidnappings, and assassinations, I live without companionship, my thwarted hopes for mankind made my violence seem futile. What were we doing to each other with our pathetic game? How will my arrest, interrogation or death change anything? When following me fails to produce more leads, will I be tortured and tell all? Betray my network? If I die, what have I done worthwhile with my life? Serve bowls of soup for atonement? Attempt to live without guilt? And if I ever confront my Stalker will he acknowledge our common humanity? Would he understand my years living under mounds of rubble? Would he feel compassion when I explained I am an Ostkinder, a child of the East, a progeny of Asiatic hordes raping and pillaging our western civilization? And how from this horror I emerged with a dream brutality cannot thwart. Yes! Change is possible. What we believe can happen will happen if we believe. If we are willing to die for renewal, for a world that can be repaired. I would insist we can raise expectations for justice, for truth. A message mankind's defeated victims cannot deny.

Pierce Barnes' knew Inga Spandau was aware of him when she lingered for an hour under the Frescos on the ceiling of the Asamkirche. Daily visits to the Hofbrauhaus, the Konigsplatz, and the Frauenkirche tried his patience. She was unpredictable. Shopping at the fruit and vegetable marketplace, haggling with vendors, she turned towards him and smiled and he anticipated her next evasive move would be a surprise. The following day he lost her as she strolled through the park and waterways of the Schloss Nymphenburg Palace. After a frantic search, he found her waiting at the gate innocent as a child. Only she was not a child but a fanatic devoted to destruction, denying value to human life. Disciplined, she lived alone without friends, family, love or sentimentality. A revolutionary for whom everything was permitted. Murder. Random killing of the innocent. No horror, no repulsive action was prohibited as she fulfilled a commitment to her concept of history. In her imagination death was victory and mass death her greatest achievement. If she portended the future God help us all! Sending her to a better world would be a civic duty.

The Carillon on Marienplatz's Town Hall ringing out the hour reminded him of other Bells on other Steeples and he did not feel homesick, just lonely, for he never had a place he called home. His spirits lifted during Fasching, the week before Lent, watching exuberant revelers dance and sing burning a life-size straw doll sacrificed for their sins proclaiming "Everything goes!" Wild women wearing masks to scare off evil spirits stormed the Town Hall running through The Plaza crowded with dancers, cutting off neckties, embracing and kissing strangers. The crowd's explosive energy overwhelmed Barnes who hesitated before joining the revelers, stepping out into the crowd of dancers, raising his arms and stamping his feet he began to dance driven by the music's compulsive beat flowing through his arms and trembling legs. Surrendering to rapture he circled and twisted and turned, eyes closed, head high, joyfully shouting, feeling a new surge of freedom. The music grew louder intensifying his ecstasy as he celebrated what it is to be alive. Exhilarated, Barnes felt gratitude for this moment floating through the dancing crowd into the arms of a tall masked partner matching her steps to his, turning and circling, crying out in a never ending flow of movement and feeling and song as the two became one. When the music stopped, her face unmasked, Inga Spandau leaned over and kissed him.

"Mr. Nobody, No where". During years in the Army Barnes often felt like a stranger temporarily inhabiting a dozen countries where he remembered only passionless one night stands serving lust and never love. "Find 'em, Feel 'em, Fuck 'em and Forget 'em" was his relationship with women who were unknown emotional territory. Here today, Gone tomorrow came to mind until Tailing Inga Spandau, following her for several weeks evoked a consuming interest in long white legs, full breasts and an inviting ass. With window shades raised and the lights on, she paraded around the room naked, turned her head towards the window and smiled as if acknowledging a devoted audience. Then a Blackout. Return tomorrow for another performance. Seeing her uncombed hair cascade down her back he imagined caressing it, thrilled by her breathtaking beauty.

What, he wondered, was her fate? Targeted Assassination? Rendition? Extreme interrogation? She provided no leads under futile surveillance made possible by immunity from a complicit government making deals with Terrorists. A Devil's bargain. Hit Rome. Attack Athens. But not Munich. Not my railroad stations, not my airports. And yes. She played him for a fool leading him by the nose like a love-sick calf.

Yes. There's all kinds of love in this world. "Bit of love, Yank, Bit of Love?" whispered hungry Prostitutes soliciting in Blackout London during the war. "A knee trembler?" they promised horny G.I.'s standing in doorways. Yes. Something to laugh about. That kind of love. Next stop the Pro Station where bored Medics insert Penicillin up now flaccid pricks. And then there's hot nights on Florida beaches, ecstatic cries, groaning, bodies rising and falling in the dark like ocean waves pounding the shore. And then there's fucking under Boardwalks while overhead Tourists strolled by unaware of the glorious passion occurring beneath their feet. Yes indeed. G.I.'s fucked in the back seat of cars, dusty Hotel rooms, cemeteries, bathrooms, and everywhere patriotic duty called to save the Free World from extinction. That kind of love.

And now there's Inga.

Intoxicated G.I.'s singing "There's nothing worse in this Universe than a woman without a man" made me shun Munich's famous Brauhaus, Inga Spandau thought, for I'm happy as I am without someone to call my own. I rejected love's romantic illusions long before being controlled by adolescent hormonal surges. And now, following me like a faithful dog, peering in my window from a flat across the street is the Tail I wag with great pleasure playing a game of attraction and repulsion. And in my solitude I become aware of my destiny to live a meaningful life. One that protests rather than accepts the presence of Evil rejecting lies as a moral duty. An act of conscience. For there are people in this world dedicated to Evil, not mistaking it for good, but knowing it as Evil, loving it as Evil. Like an angry spider the web I spin helps me destroy them. Seeing the Evil in this world I've become like the Jews in Auschwitz who put God on trial and found him guilty of murder. I find him guilty of everything wrong with our Godforsaken world. Wars. Pestilence. Hunger. Poverty. Disease. Torture. Genocide. They say God created Man in his own image. Man who kills, lies, steals, cheats, pillages, rapes and then asks for forgiveness praying for Redemption so they can die in a state of Grace and find Paradise. When I ask why? God remains silent. Blind to all the horror he bestowed on mankind. So I've stopped talking to him. I've given up on words. God is AWOL. Absent without leave. And I'm here. Yes! I'm here! All present and accounted for.

Pierce Barnes enjoyed Tailing Inga Spandau on the footpaths of the Englischer Garten crowded with walkers, joggers, and cyclists. He enjoyed the fragrance of blossoming flowers and trees spreading their leafy arms to welcome Spring. Waiting for Inga to run past his bench Barnes experienced a renewal making the landscape seem brighter and more beautiful for he was in love with a woman who would plant bombs, burn department stores, kidnap and assassinate strangers. An enemy possessed by the ecstasy of the gun dispensing death as Judge, Jury and Executioner. No one speaking a different language, worshiping another God was safe. And he wondered how we were any different believing peace and prosperity will come with our flags flying and bugles blowing sending us off to another war fought by soldiers who believe they are saving mankind? And when they no longer continue to believe this fantasy they kill themselves. A tragedy that began when Army Recruiters promised "Join the Army and see the world!" Seduced by the appeal of travel, generous benefits, and handsome uniforms patriotic High School students became John Wayne capturing Viet Cong! And if they survived combat they returned home damaged, struggling to live with haunted consciences subduing the pain of survivor guilt with drugs and alcohol, learning there's no escape from the moral injury of witnessing human suffering, adding more dead to Body Counts. In Sunday School they learned a soul can be dirtied beyond repair. No one told them about the killing, the lost arms and legs, about returning with brains that didn't work so good no more. And cheering civilians responded chanting USA! USA! USA! singing "God Bless America" to jobless, homeless heroes who now live with shadows on their souls tormented by loss, shame, guilt and regret. They went to war like heroes and came home feeling like murderers. And so Peace be with you brother. Peace be with you!

Following Inga, Barnes felt like a lonely hunter stalking his quarry through Munich's crowded streets. An urban forest inhabited by Car horns, police sirens and poisoned by the exhaust of cars and buses. No birds sang in the tree tops to accompany the sound of footsteps following him as he followed Inga and discovered he was not alone. Someone else was Tailing her. A young man in a black leather jacket and baseball cap. Barnes followed them, moving closer, and when they hesitated at the curb before crossing Ludwig Strasse, he sensed danger. Rushing towards them as the Stalker attempted to push Inga into the path of a truck, he reached out and pulled her back on to the curb as the surprised attacker turned and fled. Breathless, holding Inga in his arms, they shared the trembling excitement of the rescue prolonging a moment of happiness. Inga remained passive, embraced, her fears subsiding as she recognized Barnes. She tried speaking but words would not rise in a throat paralyzed by fear. She felt her heart racing followed by a feeling of intense gratitude. Clinging to him, she felt the reassuring beat of another heart telling her all will be well. Opening his arms, Barnes stepped back and turned away, rejecting intimacy. Inga grasped his hand, restraining him, searching for words to acknowledge her feelings. Unprepared for reconciliation, she remained a hunted fugitive. She had no other identity. And yet she also had dormant feelings of tenderness and yearning breasts that never suckled a child, never knew a lover's caress. She had become a weapon. An Engine of History. A grotesque creature who now wanted what other women wanted. Conceived by violence, she had tolerated few lovers feeling little more than a grudging acceptance of lust. Their lust, for she experienced only a release of tension. Brief dissatisfied moments telling her there must be more to this than a barren feeling as if she had dirtied her soul fucking. And now for several weeks she had displayed herself naked to an unknown voyeur. What did he think of her beauty? Did he share her excitement? And Yes! Who was he? Her Nemesis? Her handsome Stalker? Who was he?

A lifetime professional soldier who truly loved the men he shared danger with. Barnes believed there was no greater devotion than risking your life for a friend. A commitment greater than love of mother or country or passion for any woman he ever encountered. " I have your back!" expressed a love protecting men who fought our wars. Barnes had seen his band of brothers die. Called out to their shattered bodies endlessly in vain and heard only an echo of his own heart's pain. He shed tears and saluted sad little memorials of boots and helmets and dog tags in heartbreaking recognition of their sacrifice. He listened to the melancholy sound of Taps stirring the sorrow in his heart and cursed this waste of all who would never truly die as long as he remembered their smiles and songs. Their laughter at comic attempts to deny danger. He remembered the contagion of dread in the air they breathed, the empty stares of battle fatigue, vacant eyes looking off into the distance, seeing the unknown. He remembered the surprised shock of the wounded and their reluctant recognition of approaching death. And yes. He remembered all his brothers. The soldiers he loved.

What he did not remember was a woman possessing his heart as Inga did. She was no "Roll me over, Yankee soldier, roll me over, lay me down and do it again." Oh No! She was no fast romp in the hay! No one night stand! She was for real. The real thing! Love! Stirring new feelings, evoking a hunger to be touched, embraced, hugged, kissed. Wanting nothing more than to have her open up to him, to enter her or die, to ram his body into hers, to feel her tremble, groan, and cry out in the ecstasy they shared as two became one. Man, Woman, Legs, Arms, Thighs, Hips, hovering high above the earth. Flying!

Barnes had romantic fantasies of the Promised Land. Inga Spandau's bed. Following her wanderings down Munich's narrow streets and wide avenues he maintained a discrete surveillance carefully concealing their intimacy. Adhering to her routine, Inga jogged in the morning and in the afternoon ended her daily excursions at the Bijou Art Cinema watching romantic American films with Barnes seated beside her holding hands in the dark, his thigh pressed against hers, two innocent teen-agers on their first date. Some movies provided a happy escape from reality showing the verities of the human heart. Goodness, truth, beauty, loyalty, honor, trust, and above all Love's joy and happiness! But there were other films dramatizing the horrors Barnes had witnessed and could not endure seeing again. He fled from the theater. Inga followed recognizing the pain of someone tormented by Flashbacks. Recurring images reminding him of assassinations, torture and toxic interrogation techniques poisoning all they intended to save. Unable to wash away shame, he felt dirtied by what he remembered.

Uncooperative Detainees, shackled to an inclined board, heads down, faces covered with a wet cloth, struggling for breath as water poured into their mouth and nose, fighting for life, drowning, bodies shivering, legs and arms trembling, undergoing mock executions. Within fifteen to thirty seconds the water stopped pouring, postponing death with some prisoners surviving multiple Water Boardings. When supervised by a Doctor, fatalities were rare. Inflicted on battlefields, a captives' face covered with a dirty rag, water cascading from a canteen, not answering questions could be fatal. Confined for weeks alone in unlighted cells, suspended from ceiling hooks by shackled wrists, deprived of sleep, enduring extreme heat and cold, noise and silence, their naked bodies sprawled on a urine soaked floor in their own excrement, there were a few who did not break. Did not offer misinformation to end their pain.

"How was this possible? How can anyone withstand such extreme suffering?" Barnes wondered aloud. Inga Spandau set down her coffee cup and smiled. "You Americans have no monopoly on idealism. You are not the only people with convictions. Man can endure torments worse than death believing in ideas greater than personal survival." Barnes again filled his coffee cup, added cream and sugar before thoughtfully asking: "What is greater than staying alive. Surviving?"

"Having ideas worth dying for," Inga said, considering his question naïve. As the waiter set their food on the table interrupting their conversation, they remained silent. Barnes watched him return to the Kitchen wondering were they under surveillance? Has their intimacy become known?

"What are you saying?" he said, looking around the Café, studying other Patrons. Assured they were not being watched he turned to Inga as she said: "A future without wars and poverty and terror is possible if we make it happen."

Barnes smiled. Suppressed a laugh. "Such impossible dreams come and go like autumn leaves blowing in the wind."

"Building a decent world is no dream," Inga said. "You are killing and assassinating for a political fantasy," Lev replied.

"There is no alternative," Inga cried out. Desperate to be heard.

"I'm trying to end your reign of terror," Lev said.

"By water boarding?" Inga replied.

"I'm fighting for freedom for all mankind," Lev insisted.

"So am I. So am I," Inga said.

As the first rays of daylight shone through the window brightening his bedroom, Father Hussy lingered under the covers until his vision cleared. Awakening from a deep sleep he felt rested and ready to meet the demands of his vocation. After reading his morning devotions and thanking God for the gift of this new day, he rose from the bed and walked to the window to look down at the courtyard crowded with Munich's homeless drifters waiting for their daily bread and soup. His Parish doors were open to anyone in need. No refugee was ever turned away. He shaved and dressed and walked to the kitchen to assist the Cook preparing the meal, serving God by feeding the wretched survivors of Germany's defeat. Living the Gospels by never hesitating to open his door, Father Hussy recalled with gratitude the many ordinary citizens who were their brother's keeper during the war, risking their lives sheltering strangers fleeing the Gestapo. Maintaining Safe Houses across occupied Europe, the morally courageous helped thousands find sanctuary in Switzerland and Spain. A knock opening the doors of this underground Rat Line determined the life or death of Allied airmen returning to England and yes, the time of martyrs did come again, Father Hussy acknowledged as he remembered giving last rites to a brave sixteen year old Freedom Fighter, hands shackled behind his back, head held high, calmly standing in front of a blood stained execution wall, contemptuously staring at the firing squad until the moment of death. Remembering a boy who never lived to be twenty-one Father Hussy recited the ancient litany - "He gave his today so we may have our tomorrow" and he wept for this lost youth. And Yes indeed the time of martyrs did come again in occupied Europe where all citizens were prisoners and survival demanded great sacrifice. As the human spirit rose to heroic heights Father Hussy learned about the indestructibility of love. That life is a gift and preparation for Eternity, and all power attained through force, lies and deceit lead to catastrophe. After Germany surrendered Father Hussy continued his vocation supporting Aliyha Bet, the clandestine escape route from Eastern Europe transporting 100000 Jews to British Mandated Palestine. Half were intercepted, and crossing cruel and hazardous seas, in decrepit ships, 1600 drowned. 50000 survivors were then detained in DP camps in an Exodus where the cruel seas never parted but raged and stormed and sank ships while the Pharaoh's ruthless Legions flying the flag of the Royal Navy surrounded and fired upon unarmed DP's seeking peace and freedom in their promised land. And when the Iron Curtain divided Europe, Father Hussy's Church welcomed destitute escapee's hoping to live where their souls were immortal and not the property of the state. Where the human heart overcame the virulent harangues of Dictators. Where trust between one man and another prevailed. Not where by silence people gave their consent and raised the state to a level of power no government should possess. Father Hussy believed opposing injustice an act of love for life is a moral adventure in which the human spirit made a bargain with God knowing the more the soul grows old, the more it fights its fate.

At night, Father Hussy was tormented by persistent dreams that remained when he awoke. In one recurring dream he stood on the side of a wide avenue decorated with the flags and banners of many nations, his heartbeat quickening to the sound of drums and bugles as he watched a regiment of wounded war veterans march past. A grotesque parade of mutilated survivors, their hideous faces bandaged, their chest displaying decorations for valor, followed by cripples in wheel chairs, or on crutches; and jogging down the street on artificial legs, athletic veterans waved their mechanical arms to acknowledge the thunderous applause and cheers of the crowd. And when the pounding drumbeats and bugles stopped, wounded soldiers in hospital beds were rolled down the avenue by proud Honor Guards in formal dress uniforms, their hands raised to their caps in precise military salutes.

Recalling the dead in two world wars, Father Hussy no longer believed in an all-knowing, all-powerful, all-loving God. In another recurring dream wandering through a landscape of burned out tanks, shattered cannons and mounds of corpses he encountered an outraged Jesus, his face marked by suffering and sorrow, his raised left arm brandishing a clenched fist, his right hand holding an axe standing astride a fallen cross. In this recurring nightmare his Savior returned and cut down the cross of crucifixion.

A Cross of suffering we all bear, Father Hussy thought thinking about his dream. We destroy what separates us from beasts. We have wars, torture, pestilence and hunger instead of love and compassion. We murder each other for conflicting ideas of a better world, killing our children for a political cause.

In the hidden depth of our souls are memories, terrors, repulsions and fears we don't share with the world. Horrifying experiences we keep secret. We continually encounter other people with whom we have hearts, faces, and voices in common, and understanding them comes from our compassion and our ability to trust each other, losing ourselves in a love that returns our love. Through loving we find the glory of life, redemption. For cruelty is redeemed by charity, suffering by compassion and our dreams of a life worth living. Overwhelmed by new feelings, Inga Spandau and Pierce Barnes were transformed. They were now lovers seeking to know each other, thirsting for intimacy, freely giving themselves to each other confident that what they gave will be returned. They carefully maintained the charade of continued surveillance seeking romantic privacy in theaters and secluded parks aware they were being watched by unknown Tails. They knew they had departed on an impossible journey into a forbidding future giving their lives to forces beyond their control. They found peace and freedom in each other's arms when they embraced. For Inga Spandau, Barnes no longer was an overweight, over-aged professional soldier. A rude American G.I. He now seemed a romantic lover of surprising tenderness. His harsh voice and lined face became youthful arousing her love. For Barnes, Inga Spandau, the hunted criminal first seen on Mug Shots now promised passion-filled nights and an endless eternity of delights. And they also knew their joy could not continue forever.

For undocumented refugees fleeing DP camps, a most promising escape route led to Father Hussy's Church, a welcoming Safe House on the road to freedom for thousands of stateless Slave Laborers and liberated prisoners. By offering sanctuary to the desperate, the Renegade Priest defied governments refusing to meet mankind's desire for personal freedom not as a gift of benign bureaucrats but as a universal human need. He fought the corruption of the human conscience by Dictators demanding conformity as the price of survival. He was outraged by the horror wrought by their unlimited power creating Concentration camps, Slave Labor camps, Death Marches, and Population Transfers killing millions who marched off to war applauding charismatic Leaders pursuing fantasies of national glory. Armed with food, shelter and a Volkswagen Bus transporting refugees across borders, Father Hussy fought another kind of war offering a new life to survivors rising from the dead. Opposing Evil and promoting what was good was his true vocation and when Inga and Barnes came to his Church and asked to marry he could not refuse.

Driving through the Oberbayern province to the Austrian border, they followed an ancient 14th century Roman Trade Route that once carried the spices and exotic goods of the Levant to Europe. They drove towards Germany's highest mountain, the Zugspitze dominating an Alpine scene of snow covered peaks and green valleys. For a Flatlander from Kansas the majestic Alps evoked a feeling of awe at their overwhelming grandeur. As they climbed a high mountain pass their Volkswagen engine coughed and sputtered losing power in the thin air. Father Hussy carefully drove the hazardous road leading Barnes and Inga to their next Safe House. To freedom. For Father Hussy Freedom was a gift he offered to anyone fleeing Tyranny.

Travelling together, anticipating the future, Father Hussy felt a powerful emotional current flowing between the embracing lovers, holding hands, touching, kissing, silently expressing what they felt for each other. For the old Priest being truly and deeply in love was one of life's great mysteries defying rational understanding. He was often moved to tears when he encountered lovers showing passion.

Yes. There was more to life than loving God. Much more, fenced off by a wall of celibacy for Father Hussy.

As their bus reached the summit of the mountain pass beginning a slow descent down into the valley below, the bright light of the rising sun fell upon their faces and Father Hussy realized the lovers were both happy and sad and had been crying in their sleep like children inhabiting a world they did not yet understand. As the shadows of the night filled with the golden rays of a new day, Inga awoke and turned to Father Hussy and smiled. "Guten Morgen" she said. "Another glorious day". Father Hussy nodded and said: "Every day is truly a gift of God." Inga did not reply. Staring out the window, her face glowing with exuberant joy, she felt a happiness that was almost too much to bear. Sighing, she raised her hand, and pointed at the snow covered mountains towering above them, unable to find words expressing her feelings she began to sing.

She sang a song only lovers sing, a song of hearts quite young, a song of youth, filled with truth, a melody quite free.

NELLIS USAF BASE, NEVADA

Lt. Roger Smith expected another monotonous day at work. After finishing a breakfast of toast, eggs, orange juice, and two cups of black coffee he kissed his wife and son good morning before driving to a remote Top Secret Air Force base in the Nevada desert. For the next eight hours he sat in a comfortable leather arm chair in an air conditioned Trailer watching a TV monitor piloting a remote Drone 15000 feet above a distant land. His daily mission was tracking vehicles carrying suspected terrorist, smugglers, and criminals carefully monitored, and then assessed for further action at a higher level of authority. When ordered to fire, Lt. Smith zoomed in on his target and guided by computed distance, direction and range, he launched a Hellfire missile in this new way of warfare where Targeted Assassination became a civic duty, and Kill Sites were carefully limited to remote rural areas to minimize collateral damage to innocent civilians. A lonely mountain road certainly qualified as a place to attack.

His Action Report that day recorded the destruction of a Volkswagen bus travelling the highway from Garmisch to within ten Kilometers of the Austrian border. Pierce Barnes, Inga Spandau and Father Hussy were instantly vaporized, their torn body parts, brains, organs, and limbs vanishing forever in a cloud of dust, smoke, and small metal fragments forever resting unmarked on the roadside as a mound of rusted junk.

Lt. Roger Smith looked forward to the end of his workday when he would sign his daily Log book and drive to the Little League baseball field to watch his son pitch several innings of a hotly contested ball game. He was proud of the boy's unexpected talent. A promising future in professional athletics was possible if nourished at an early age. Lt. Roger Smith regretted the lost years, the years that would never come again when stationed overseas he missed watching his son grow up. Returning home between Tours he would encounter a different child and worked hard to renew the bond of love between them. He had no doubt his son always missed him, and having an absentee father was difficult for a boy who never complained accepting as normal the loneliness of a one parent childhood. Someday his son would understand his father was safeguarding his future, serving the high purpose of insuring his opportunity to live safe and secure in freedom and prosperity. The high price of freedom must be paid and he and his son were meeting that obligation. And yes! Someday his son would understand and forgive not always having a father around when needed.

So when Lt. Roger Smith thought about his work he only thought about his son. He did not consider the consequences of what he was doing. He was the final actor, the one who pressed the trigger at the end of a series of decisions by Commanders who analyzed, assessed and selected High Value Targets. He was fighting a war in which sudden terror from the sky was a brutal demonstration of government power. He was one of a patriotic group of good men killing by remote control, close-up, in real time, seeing the blood and severed body parts, intimately witnessing unspeakable human carnage, emotionally disturbing. Not to be thought about.

THE NEGEV DESERT

As if ordained by God, flowing rivers, wide oceans or high mountains create natural borders. In the Middle East boundaries were often arbitrary lines drawn by Diplomats representing triumphant Colonial powers with no regard for inhabitants. In 1923, the Hashemite Kingdom of Jordan, ruled by King Abdullah, achieved independence from the British mandate and immediately established national borders. For more than two thousand miles, imaginary lines in the sand guarded by barbed wire and checkpoints asserted Jordan's sovereignty over a desert nation. In our divided world, disputed borders caused centuries of warfare, ethnic cleansing, genocide and population transfers. Bedouin smugglers crossing these borders supported their families buying and selling contraband goods in Arabian black markets. For Ahamed Haddad and Baruch Lev, crossing into Jordan, reaching Aqaba, the gateway to the Red Sea promised freedom and safety.

A barrier of barbed wire and a minefield along the Wadi Arava, the southern outlet of the Dead Sea, defended Jordan's western border. Arriving at night, the Bedouins herded their sheep into the minefield to clear a safe path thru the wire. Cutting an opening in the fence, the Caravan followed the path of exploded mines and dead sheep to cross the border safely. Alerted by the detonated mines, Jordanian soldiers raced to the site to ambush the Bedouins in brief and bloody firefights. Attacking in the dark firing, at unseen intruders, reluctant to suffer casualties, often bribed by the Bedouins, the soldiers disengaged after a few rounds of gunfire to falsely report another successful victory protecting their homeland.

Fleeing across the desert to escape the vengeance of his organization Ahamed Haddad felt estranged from friends and family. Now without his Brotherhood of Freedom

Fighters he struggled to accept his fate. Riding all night, kept awake by the discomfort of the saddle he studied the stars overhead to divert his mind from his thoughts. His many regrets. Actions he would now do differently were remembered not with pride but with shame. As his mind filled with his past he knew remorse had no cure, no way of assessing good and evil, justice and injustice. Choices he would live or die by. Refusing to allow the decapitation of Baruch Lev, his former enemy, now a friend, Haddad realized Arabs and Israelis must learn to love one another, or die. If he escaped to live a new life he would teach love is more powerful than death, compromise greater than hatred, and freedom does not come free. And certainly the words, making peace possible would come from God. Allah Akbar !

Baruch Lev knew he would cross this border and never return. Never return to betraying the Zionist dream of living in peace, truth, justice and respect for the opinion of mankind and the rule of law. A dream that was once realized when the founding leaders respected human rights. A dream defended in five wars by 20 thousand dead whose sacrifice had been betrayed by unworthy men. Baruch Lev would abandon a country obsessed with Biblical fantasies. A society driven by greed, led by secular and religious fanatics. Baruch Lev resolved to find sanctuary abroad advocating a return to the old Zionist dream. He would revive the eternal verities of more than five thousand years. He would discard his uniform, lay down his weapons, and no longer serve a state that lost its way. He would be his own man.

Lev recognized the sound of machine guns firing at him. High pitched whines, a staccato series of bursts coming out of the dark, flashes of light on either side of the ambush. He smacked his riding crop against the flank of the Camel as he felt a hard fist pounding his chest. Shock waves travelling through his body drove the air out of his lungs leaving him breathless. "Oh No!" he shouted. "Oh No!" he groaned as he collapsed falling from the saddle. The machine gun fire intensified as the Caravan ran through the ambush. Sprawled in the sand, Lev felt life ebbing, a receding tide of energy and spirit pouring from the sucking wound in his chest as he lay on the ground face up, struggling for breath. Looking up at the constellations overhead he believed his life had not been wasted. Turning an enemy into a loved and beloved friend is always a Mitzvah. A good deed. Then the gunfire stopped and darkness blotted out the stars.

When the gunfire ceased, Haddad and Sheikh Hussein, seeing the empty saddle on Lev's camel dismounted and walked back to the ambush site. Guided by the moans and cries of the wounded sprawled on the side of the track, they found a safe passage through the minefield. As a crescent moon emerged from behind a cloud illuminating the scene, Haddad, grateful at how few casualties they suffered was unaware the soldiers had been bribed to withdraw. He shouted "Insha' Allah! God is Great!" explaining their luck as the border was now open to them. His heart also opened in a new way accepting his love for Baruch Lev until it seemed his whole world was filled with love. Love as a primal force of human nature. The source of enduring loyalty, justice, friendship and trust. He no longer doubted the existence of God. The God of love. The driving force of history. A love that overpowers people and redirects their lives. Searching for his friend, Haddad was filled with an overpowering happiness he had never known before. A happiness he could only express by shouting "Allah Akbar!"

As a moving cloud covered the crescent moon, seeing Lev lying off the side of the track, Haddad stepped out into the darkness towards his friend. He felt the uncoiled spring under foot release the land mine propelling it chest high and knowing his fate, Haddad was grateful to have lived long enough to have discovered the indestructibility of love.

Attracted by the sound of the exploding land mine, Sheikh Heussein found Haddad's shattered body beyond salvation. Nearby, he discovered Baruch Lev bleeding to death. He knelt beside him to bind up his wounds and raising his eyes to heaven said: "Another good son of Abraham will soon find his way to Paradise."

THE PRIMINISTER, ONE YEAR LATER

Occupied by peaceful demonstrators, the Plaza below the Prime Minister's office window was a crowded tent city of flags and signs and voices pleading "Free Baruch Lev". Low flying Helicopters hovered above the scene, the nerve shattering roar of their rotating blades intensifying the threat of riot. A cordon of soldiers guarded the entrances to the Plaza. Entertained by chanting and singing students, the soldiers removed their gas masks smiling and laughing and applauding the surging crowd. The demonstration's leaders shouted into megaphones inciting a series of rhythmic responses to their questions: "What do you want?" and "When do you want it?" The angry audience roared back - "Free Baruch Lev!" and "Free him Now!" as they shouted and danced performing for the TV cameras broadcasting their demands to the world.

The Prime Minister walked from the window, shook his head and turned to General Posner, his voice trembling as he said: "Bleeding hearts and do-gooders demand the impossible. The Terrorists are playing with a bargaining chip who may be dead. Lev's last video was over a year ago. How can we negotiate without proof he is alive? Let those kids sing their hearts out. I will never negotiate!"

General Posner, looked down at the Plaza awed by the raucous demonstration. He turned to the Prime Minister and paused a moment controlling his anger. "Lev is of no value to the Terrorists dead. Their threat to decapitate him was never real. They are playing a waiting game of now you see him now you don't. You must wait for their next move."

"And if we don't hear from them?" the Prime Minister demanded . "What then? How much longer can we tolerate mob rule in the streets? Anarchy? This situation is unacceptable. Those damn kids are helping the Terrorists.

The world is watching while we do nothing, losing our deterrence credibility. We have no choice but to pre-empt their dirty game."

General Posner turned from the window and challenged the Prime Minister. "What do you mean pre-empt? What are you saying?"

"That we officially declare Baruch Lev dead, Bury him with military honors with guns and waving flags and a tombstone inscribed with an eloquent tribute to a fallen warrior."

General Posner remained silent. Shocked. Surprised. Searching for a reply. "Where is his body? You can't bury an empty coffin."

"Our Morgue is filled with unclaimed dead," the Prime Minister explained as General Posner struggled to regain his composure.

"What if he reappears and makes a mockery of your fancy burial?" General Posner asked demanding an answer.

"That is not possible,' the Prime Minister insisted. "That will never happen."

"How can you be so sure?" General Posner shouted. "You've been wrong before."

"Lev is dead" replied the Prime Minister.

"Is that an opinion or a fact?" General Posner demanded.

"Last year a Satellite photographed a Firefight on the Jordanian border a few miles north of Aqaba," the Prime Minister explained. "A caravan of Bedouin smugglers were ambushed by the Jordanian Army with many casualties. Lev died fleeing to another country."

"A Satellite picture?" General Posner said critically. "Not exactly reliable confirmation."

"We had something else," the Prime Minister explained. "In an Aqaba Bazaar our agent found a gold chain and Star of David identified as belonging to Baruch Lev."

The continuous roar of Helicopters circling low over the Plaza continued to threaten the demonstrators rhythmically chanting -- "Free Baruch Lev! Free him now!" General Posner shook his head, walked to the window and pointed at the angry crowd. "What will you tell them,", he asked. "Nothing," replied the Prime Minister.

"Nothing? You will say nothing?" General Posner said. Enraged. "You will remain silent with the entire world condemning us because of your refusal to negotiate!"

"I will stand by my decision," replied the Prime Minister. "Forever!"

"You will be impeached," General Posner cried out. "Impeached!"

"I believe History will judge me fairly," The Prime Minister replied without emotion.

"No one will defend your deceptions," General Posner insisted. "No one!"

The Prime Minister nodded and smiled. A man at peace with himself. "My enemies have always been as numerous as the stars in the sky. I will resign knowing I have done what is best for my country."

EPILOGUE

In years to come, the most popular Hikaaya or narrative sung by Bedouin storytellers, was the "Legend of Abu Lev" the Israeli soldier who was born again as a Bedouin. Poets honoring him recited hours of eloquent poetry, delightful Shi'r that stirred the hearts and minds of the illiterate telling how Abu Lev defended Bedouin ownership of land they inhabited for centuries. Poets sang of how his argument before the nation's highest Court restored Bedouin rights as citizens of a country they once defended with their lives. They told how Sheikh Hussein brought Abu Lev back from the dead, restored him to health as he lay dying of his wounds to live and go forth to defend the Bedouin's traditional way of life. A culture that would be lost forever. They told how he protected Bedouin water and grazing rights, fought confiscations of their land, prevented evictions and relocations and dispossessions compelling the government to recognize the existence of ancient Bedouin villages. And to keep alive the history of their people, Bedouin Poets and Storytellers told of "Tikkun olam", -- how another Jew attempted to repair the world.

About the Author

After a 42 year career as a writer-director of many award-winning films and television programs, Norman Weissman has written three novels and a Memoir. Determined to oppose the silence in which Lies become history, the author makes his reply in art to tell all he has witnessed filming here and overseas. He lives in Connecticut with his wife Eveline.

Also by Norman Weissman

Acceptable losses   A Novel

Snapshots USA (An American Family Album)   A Novel

My Exuberant Voyage   A Memoir

Oh Palestine

CPSIA information can be obtained
at www.ICGtesting.com
Printed in the USA
FFOW03n2014260315
12168FF